The Islamic Question
in Middle East Politics

The Islamic Question in Middle East Politics

Alan R. Taylor

Westview Press
Boulder and London

To Hisham Sharabi

My first mentor
and friend of many years

Copyright © 1988 by Westview Press, Inc.

Published in 1988 in the United States of America by Westview Press, Inc.; Frederick A. Praeger, Publisher; 5500 Central Avenue, Boulder, Colorado 80301

Library of Congress Cataloging-in-Publication Data
Taylor, Alan R.
The Islamic question in Middle East politics / Alan R. Taylor.
    p. cm.
  Bibliography: p.
  Includes index.
  ISBN 0-8133-7500-2
  ISBN 0-8133-7588-6 (pbk.)
    1. Islam and politics—Middle East. 2. Middle East—Politics and government—1945- . 3. Islamic fundamentalism—Middle East.
I. Title.
BP63.A4M538 1988
320.5′0956—dc19   87-27139
                                                                       CIP

Printed and bound in the United States of America

∞ The paper used in this publication meets the requirements of the American National Standard for Permanence of Paper for Printed Library Materials Z39.48-1984.

10   9   8   7   6   5   4   3   2

Contents

4-15-91

Preface

The intention of this book is to develop to its logical conclusion a particular interpretation of the secular nationalist and Islamic neofundamentalist responses to the decline of traditional sociopolitical order in the Middle East. My primary argument is that secular nationalism as an institution borrowed from the West has in many respects failed to create a more viable political system in part because it was insufficiently liberal; however, the attempt to establish a better order by resort to a radical repoliticized Islam has also been unsuccessful because it did not include in its doctrine the humanistic aspects of the Islamic tradition. These two movements will be examined in depth, with particular reference to the relevance of Islam in the present situation. The Islamic question in Middle East politics concerns what role Islam can and should play in the reconstruction of the area's ideological orientation and institutional framework. This is an especially important issue, given the current dislocation in the coherence of existing belief systems. The way it is addressed will have repercussions of major consequence.

The book provides a useful overview of the origins, development, and eventual encounters of secular nationalism and the various manifestations of the Islamic reform movement. The respective ideological systems will be analyzed in some detail, along with a history of relevant events. The major focus, however, will be on the elaboration of the interpretive theme. The scope of the book is restricted to the Middle East—Turkey, Iran, and the Arab states.

The methodological approach stresses historical analysis. A number of premises underlie the application of this technique to this particular topic. The first is that the modern reconstructionist movements in the Middle East have been dealing either affirmatively or negatively with the Islamic heritage, the historical base of the area's culture. The trauma of modernization stems partly from ambivalent attitudes toward the powerful influence of Islamic tradition, which shaped the past and maintains continuity in the present. Though it is still a major determinant of behavioral patterns, Western modes of thought and action have also become part of the system of social dynamics and are regarded by many as more useful and appropriate in the contemporary world. The interaction of tradition and modernization is best understood through the use of historical methods, though the topic also falls within the domain of the cultural anthropologist.

Another premise is that the changes in social, economic, and political structures brought on by the colonization of the Middle East had a major impact on the area's orientation. The dislocation of traditional class roles and the dramatically altered relationship with the West uprooted the old system of loyalties, authority, and collective goals and replaced it with a new set of values and priorities. A historical approach is the most appropriate methodology for analyzing this kind of transition because it emphasizes the interrelationship of past and present and of events and culture.

The final premise is that the historical approach is particularly useful in interpreting the symbols and myths through which individuals and groups explain to themselves what they believe in and what they are putting into action. This approach is naturally disposed to looking at the entirety of human experience as opposed to a particular dimension. The ideologies of secular nationalism and the various forms of Islamic reconstructionism represent responses to a historical development requiring a reassessment of tradition and a consideration of innovation. This is a very disturbing process psychologically and leads to formulations about Islam and Westernization that are often both subjective and selective. A byproduct of the modernization crisis, such belief systems can be evaluated qualitatively only by reference to concepts that originated in other times or places and were then reinterpreted to address problems arising from contemporary circumstances in the Middle East. Because it concerns change and the response to it, the entire process is by nature historical.

With respect to the terminology used for contemporary Islamic movements, "Islamic modernism" connotes the school of thought associated with the late nineteenth-century Egyptian reformer, Muhammad Abduh. Though advocating an Islamic revival inspired by the model of early Islam, this Islamic modernism was also cosmopolitan in orientation because its founders had been influenced by the European intellectual currents of the time. "Islamic fundamentalism" refers to the conservative approach to reform, usually literalist and puritanical, exemplified by the Wahhabi movement and the subsequent Saudi monarchy in the Arabian Peninsula. "Islamic neofundamentalism" is used interchangeably with "Islamic resurgence" or "Islamic militancy" to refer to the more recent movement that in most cases seeks to repoliticize Islam and establish an Islamic government, while calling for the eradication of most or all Western cultural and political influences in Islamic societies.

The transliteration of words and names in Middle East languages represents a combination of common usage and a simplified version of the academic method. Arabic, Persian, and Turkish words and names are generally spelled in the manner used by contemporary scholars in those languages but without diacritical marks or nonphonetic endings. Popular spellings have been employed for such common names as "Abdul Nasser," "Hussein," and "Maghreb." If individuals cited prefer a particular transliteration of their personal names, such as "Mohammed," these are also used in referring to them.

I thank Professor John O. Voll, Christopher S. Taylor, Dr. George Atiyeh, Dr. Mohammad Hasan Hosseinbor, and Malise Ruthven for their kind assistance in reviewing the manuscript and making helpful suggestions.

Alan R. Taylor

1

Origins of the Islamic Question: An Overview

The emergence of militant, neofundamentalist Islam as a significant political force in the Middle East following the 1967 war has provoked a variety of reactions and attempts to explain its ultimate meaning. Within the region, apologists and critics of the resurgence movements have developed elaborate arguments to support or condemn their activities and doctrines. In the West, the public, the press, and even most governments have not gone far beyond the stage of characterizing the militants as a Middle Eastern version of the World War II Japanese kamikaze pilots, deemed hostile and dangerous because of their dedicated "fanaticism." Scholars in several countries have been trying to develop more sophisticated interpretations.

The sudden appearance of a radical form of repoliticized Islam came as a shock to many because of its deviation from established norms and its unexpected success in some cases. The overthrow of the shah's regime in Iran under the leadership of Ayatollah Khomeini, the assassination of Anwar Sadat in Egypt by members of the Jihad organization, the confrontations between Asad and Islamic militants in Syria, and the exploits of extremist Shiites in Lebanon aroused deep concern in both the Middle East and the West. A new and unpredictable variable seemed to have been launched in the mainstream of Middle East politics.

The origins and import of contemporary Islamic resurgence are best understood from an historical perspective. This phenomenon is actually a recent manifestation of a complex pattern of reactions to the decline of Islamic society and institutions in the Middle East, stemming partly from and then accelerated by the economic, political, and cultural intrusion of the West. The political cohesiveness of the Islamic empire had actually ended by the tenth century, though Islam continued indefinitely as a formidable cultural tradition periodically reaffirmed by movements of revival and reconstruction. Nevertheless, its intellectual resilience became less pronounced in the late medieval period, and though there was continuing creativity, scholarly activity was with increasing frequency based on reference to the legitimized sources of theological, legal, and sociopolitical theory. The establishment of the Ottoman Empire represented the revival of a Middle Eastern Islamic political imperium, but its cultural achievements did not match those of the Abbasid period. This decreased the capacity to deal with internal and external problems once the Ottoman system had become dysfunctional in the sense that its political and economic institutions were no longer fully operative.

In the seventeenth century the decline of the Ottoman Empire and the gap in performance ability between the Middle East and a newly galvanized Europe became clearly evident. The Ottoman sultan turned over the running of state affairs to members of the talented Köprülü family, a succession of whom served as grand vizier from 1656 to 1697 and tried to revitalize the administrative system and the military establishment. However, the abortive second siege of Vienna in 1683 led to a prolonged war with an alliance of European powers and the eventual defeat of the Ottoman forces in 1699.

The eclipse of the Ottoman Empire extended over more than two centuries following the end of the war with the European alliance. By the nineteenth century, the once invincible Ottoman imperium had become the "sick man of Europe," a prize to be won in the rivalry for colonial aggrandizement among Great Britain, Russia, France, and Austria. For the Ottomans, the "Eastern Question" was a humiliating and traumatic experience in which their political and territorial sovereignty was progressively diminished and partition of the entire Middle East became inevitable. Neighboring Iran, which had become a powerful state at the beginning of the sixteenth century, suffered the same fate and in 1907 was partitioned into zones of influence between Great Britain and Russia.

These untoward developments generated a quest to rescue the besieged Islamic order in the Middle East from the designs of the colonizing powers. Concern over the major alteration in the power structure in what William McNeill has called the "Eurasian ecumene" actually began much earlier. The European challenge had since the sixteenth century confronted most non-Western societies with a crisis in which traditional cultures were subjected to the test of utility. From the beginning, the two responses to the problem in the Middle East were either "a rigorous reassertion of the pristine truths of religion, as preached by Mohammed himself" or attempts "to appropriate those aspects of European civilization which seemed responsible for the Europeans' success."[1]

These schools of thought on what form and direction the needed sociopolitical adjustments should take were the dominant responses to the problem of decline in the late nineteenth century. The first advocated direct borrowing from the Western models of secular culture and nationalism, the presumption being that the only effective way to meet the challenge of Western political and cultural intrusion was to adopt, at least in part, those institutions that had made the European powers so irresistibly powerful. Also implicit in this approach was the premise that Western secular civilization was innately superior to the established Islamic culture of the Middle East.

The second school of thought held that the only viable solution to the problem was the reconstruction of Islam itself. The underlying theory here was that contemporary Islam is a degenerate form of the original and that the only way to revitalize it is to reopen the doors of *ijtihad* (rational judgment) and overhaul the existing institutional structure, using early Islam and the best aspects of Western sociopolitical practice as the models. The relative roles of these two very different models were never adequately defined. This ambiguity left a significant uncertainty as to whether "Islamic modernism," as this doctrine of change came to be known, was essentially more "Islamic" than "modern" (in the Western sense) or vice versa.

During the nineteenth and early twentieth centuries, the advocates of Westernization became the principal architects of the revised order. This was almost certainly the result of the perceived utilitarian advantages this line of development seemed to entail. Muhammad Ali, the virtually autonomous governor of Egypt from 1805 to 1849, was one of the earliest modernizers. His reforms were superficial, however, in the sense that they were restricted to improving technique and administration without liberalizing the political system or changing established cultural patterns. The thrust of change in the Ottoman system was also initially cosmetic, a factor graphically symbolized in two equestrian portraits of the reformer sultan, Mahmud II (1809–1839). The first, painted in the earlier part of his reign, showed him wearing the traditional Islamic turban. The second, done after he had begun to institute his reforms, depicts him in full European military regalia.

The subsequent Tanzimat (reorganization) of the 1839–1876 period introduced more significant modifications, which included systematic borrowing from Western institutions. This approach considerably altered the established Islamic structure, though it fell short of converting the empire into a constitutional monarchy. The Young Ottoman movement, which became active in 1865, sought to bring the Tanzimat to its logical conclusion through the promulgation of a constitution. Successful for a brief period in 1876–1877, the constitution was suspended by the new sultan, Abdul Hamid II. It was finally restored after the 1908 coup executed by the Young Turks, who had succeeded the Young Ottomans as champions of constitutionalism. A similar movement emerged in Iran in the early 1900s, leading to the formation of a constitutional monarchy in 1906. In this case, the experiment lasted only five years.

Islamic modernism in the Turkish part of the empire was developed by some of the Young Ottoman thinkers. The most prominent of these was Namik Kemal, who sought to create a synthesis of Islamic law and Western parliamentary practice based on the concepts of natural law and popular sovereignty.[2] An even more comprehensive theory of Islamic modernism was elaborated in Egypt by Jamal al-Din al-Afghani and Muhammad Abduh in the 1870s and 1880s.[3] Using the age of the *salaf* (early Muslim generations) as a model for change in the present, they called for the recreation of the climate of free inquiry that had existed in the illustrious periods of Islamic history. This climate would enable contemporary Muslims to reinterpret Islam, implicitly even with reference to the modern West within proper bounds, in order to meet the challenges of modern times. Though the *salafiyya* movement, as it came to be known, generated an interest in change and reform in the Arab world, it had little direct political impact. It also never really resolved the problem of how to use an idealized inaugural period of Islamic history as a guide for the present following centuries of malpractice.

Though the political reforms that ended with the Young Turk regime did not save the Ottoman Empire from extinction after World War I, the Western concept of nationalism began to emerge as the new ideological orientation of Middle East politics. Ziya Gökalp formulated a doctrine of Turkism to replace the moribund Ottomanism of the Young Turks, and it became the guiding principle of the Turkish republic fashioned by Mustafa Kemal Atatürk after the war. In the Arab provinces, regional versions of Arab nationalism became the basis of the liberation movement from British rule in Egypt and the anti-Ottoman separatism in the Fertile Crescent. Not until the 1930s was the broader pan-Arab nationalism introduced by Sati al-Husri and others. Nationalism was never very clearly defined in Iran, but it was implicit in the constitutional movement of 1906 and to some extent in the programs of the Pahlevi dynasty after 1925.

The rise of nationalism as an immensely popular political creed and the theoretical raison d'être of many post-Ottoman regimes was a revolutionary development of major proportions. Based on the European model, it was highly secular in character and marked a radical departure from Middle Eastern political tradition. It had nothing whatever in common with the concept of the transregional Islamic community (*umma*) and only a remote connection with the notions of component peoples (*qawm*) and distinct geographical entities (*watan*) within the Islamic empires of the past. Moreover, it stood in stark contrast with the religious principles of Islam by assigning highest priority to the welfare and aspirations of particular ethnic and/or territorial groups deemed to have distinct "national" identities.

Indeed, for many of its adherents nationalism became a new article of faith, something on the order of a secular religion dedicated to the higher destiny of special peoples. In this respect, it entailed what Arnold Toynbee referred to as the "idolization of a parochial community."[4] Though Islam was never explicitly renounced, it was reduced in many cases to a facet of national culture. The pan-Arab nationalists went so far as to characterize Muhammad as the founder of the Arab nation, thus reinterpreting Islam as an ethnic political movement.

The appeal of nationalism arose largely from its function as a liberating force in opposition to foreign domination, whether British, French, or Turkish. Increasingly, it achieved practical results, engendering a new sense of identity and patriotism. Islamic modernism, on the other hand, remained theoretical and seemed to have little relevance in terms of resolving the immediate problems of internal dysfunction and external intervention. Despite the favorable reputation of people like Muhammad Abduh, the intellectualism of the late nineteenth-century Islamic reform doctrines could not win the broad populist backing that was easily recruited by the nationalist ideologies.

Ultimately, nationalism became the basis of most post-Ottoman political systems in the Middle East. The Turkish Republic, which marked the culmination of a century of Ottoman political Westernization, became the classic example of the secular state. The abolition of the sultanate-caliphate in 1922–1924 symbolized the break with the past. The new Pahlevi regime in Iran, also established in the 1920s, followed a similar pattern but retained the traditional trappings and power of the Persian monarchy while introducing a wide range of Western institutions and practices. The implicit contradictions of this combination ev ntually led to the overthrow of the dynasty more than fifty years later.

In the Arab world, regional nationalism was the dominant political theme in Egypt, the Fertile Crescent, and the Maghreb after World War I, though it took much longer for these movements to establish independence from European control. Not until after the World War II did the component states begin to achieve genuine independence. Moreover, the boundaries in the Fertile Crescent and to a lesser extent in the Maghreb had been determined by the preceding colonial administrative jurisdictions. A further complication was the British commitment, never precisely defined, to the establishment of a "Jewish national home" in Palestine. This commitment threatened to lead to the creation of an alien settler state at the juncture between the Arab countries of Africa and Asia. These various hindrances impaired the nation-building process of the regional nationalist regimes and stimulated the emergence of the more doctrinaire ideology of pan-Arab nationalism.

Whatever the circumstances, nationalism in practice began to run into difficulties as early as the 1930s. The systems in Turkey and Iran were less troubled than those in the Arab world, largely because the former had established independence at an early stage and because they had a relatively clear idea of the territorial limits of the homeland they represented and of the national aims they were seeking to achieve. Yet both were essentially directive in the way they imposed their modernization programs, and in certain respects they could be considered authoritarian. Though Atatürk was an extremely popular leader, Turkey was still a one-party state and there was no possibility of challenging the theory and policies of Kemalism. Also, Atatürk was a former military officer, and the army was always prepared to intervene, if necessary, to preserve the principles upon which the state had been founded. Reza Pahlevi also came from a military background and ruled Iran as a kind of "enlightened despot." He held on to the traditional trappings of centralization, considering this approach to be the only way he could modernize and secularize the country.

Nationalism in the Arab countries was focused on the struggle for independence from the vestiges of colonial rule during the interwar period. The leadership enjoyed broad popular support at this time, but the dominant parties were also being transformed into oligarchic elites, mostly representative of landed and upper-middle-class interests. By the eve of World War II, they were discredited in the eyes of the masses, the newly emerging intelligentsia, and large segments of the younger generation. The old slogans of patriotism and secular liberalism lost their earlier appeal, and the growing opposition was searching for a more credible interpretation of the nationalist idea.

Although after World War II, the nationalist order underwent certain changes, in most cases these led to further complications rather than a resolution of the problems apparent in the 1930s. Turkish politics became a two-party system in 1946, and the new Democratic party took over in 1950. The regime was ousted by military intervention a decade later, however, because it had engaged in unconstitutional practices in its attempt to remain in power. The Turkish political structure became increasingly fragile over the following twenty years, leading to further interventions by the army in 1971 and 1980. The second of these coups restored stability but made the army an integral part of the reconstructed system. Dubbed "disciplined democracy," it curtailed a number of traditional freedoms and established tighter controls over the country.

Iran entered a period of uncertainty after World War II, followed by a revolutionary trend first expressed in the transitory revolution of 1951–

1953 and then gathering more momentum in the 1960s and 1970s. In the earlier period, when Muhammad Musaddiq's National front was the dominant opposition group, the major issue was foreign economic and political intervention in Iran. The "Western connection" remained a serious question during the following two decades, but the increasingly repressive consolidation of power by the new shah, Muhammad Reza Pahlevi, became a more important subject of debate. By the mid-1970s, a formidable revolutionary movement with strong Islamic undertones confronted the shah's regime and eventually brought about its overthrow in 1979.

In the nationalist countries of the Arab world, parties and military cliques representing a revisionist interpretation of nationalism began to take over the reins of government in the 1950s. The successful revolution executed by the Free Officers in Egypt in July 1952 and the subsequent rise to power of the charismatic Gamal Abdul Nasser were the most dramatic in a series of events that changed the political character of several major Arab countries. The emergence of the Baath party as a new force in Syrian politics after 1955 and the overthrow of the monarchy in Iraq in 1958 set the stage for a Baathist succession in both countries in 1963.

Pan-Arabism and Arab socialism became the cardinal ideals of the new ideology of nationalism. The psychological mood that spread through much of the Arab world was one of anticipation that the fulfillment of unrealized aspirations was close at hand. These were heady days, when such events as the Syrian-Egyptian merger of 1958 seemed like the beginning of Arab unification and of government based on high principles. This union would, it was thought, mark the end of foreign intervention and of the Israeli state in Palestine, symbols of the failure of the preceding regimes.

The euphoria proved to be short lived. Syria withdrew from the United Arab Republic in September 1961. The 1962 revolution in Yemen initiated a civil war in which Egypt and Saudia Arabia became involved as supporters of the opposing sides. The talks in 1963 aimed at exploring approaches to unity between the Nasser government and the newly installed Baathist regimes in Syria and Iraq ended in failure and led to bickering among states that professed to be "revolutionary" and progressive. The first Arab summit conference in 1964 produced only meager results. The pessimism generated by these untoward events was turned into despair by the massive Arab defeat in the June 1967 war.

The victory of Israel and its acquisition of Sinai, the West Bank, Gaza, and the Golon Heights became a watershed in the history of the contemporary Arab world. The popularity of Nasserism as an ideology began to decline, and Nasser himself placed increasing emphasis on the primacy of Egyptian interests. Indeed, serious support for pan-Arabism diminished progressively in most Arab countries. Egyptians also started to question the ability of Arab socialism to improve measurably the quality of life through its visionary economic programs. Furthermore, they were certain that Nasser had not found a satisfactory way of dealing with the ever more difficult problem of Israel, which now included occupation of Egyptian terrorritory. The general disillusionment made people more aware of the shortcomings of the Nasserist system, including its intolerance of political opposition within the country.

The Baathist regimes in Syria and Iraq had similar difficulties in preserving their credibility. In February 1966, the military wing of the party executed a coup, leading initially to the repressive government of Salah Jadid and then in 1970 to the more moderate but nonetheless tenacious dictatorship of Hafiz al-Asad. The Baath in Iraq opposed these Syrian regimes as deviating from the principles of the party. Yet when Hasan al-Bakr and Saddam Hussein came to power in Baghdad in 1968, they monopolized power and dealt ruthlessly with opposition in very much the same way as their counterparts had in Damascus. Though they paid lip service to pan-Arabism and justice, both branches of the party carried on a relentless rivalry with each other while keeping tight authoritarian control over their respective countries through the auspices of loyal and carefully selected sectarian elites. In terms of ideological substance, the Baath had ceased to exist, though the trappings of Baathism were used to preserve power and serve as a cover for various kinds of political abuse and malpractice.

In response to the manifest failures of Nasserism and Baathism, those who still believed in secular nationalism sought a different revision of the basic doctrine that would make it more broadly acceptable. An attempt was made to divest it of idealism and extravagant aspirations, to bring it down to earth by making it pragmatic without being cynical. Anwar Sadat became the principal architect of this new interpretation of the nationalist idea. The major themes of his administration were to strengthen the private sector of the Egyptian economy, officially discard the pan-Arab objective, develop a close working relationship with the United States as opposed to the Soviet Union, and bring an end to the dispute with Israel, now deemed obsolete. In a series of policy decisions, he instituted an *infitah* ("open door") policy and revived the earlier Egyptian nationalist orientation of the country. He also cemented ties with the United States by cooperating with Henry Kissinger's peace initiative and pursuing the process of negotiations that began with the Camp David accords and ended with the Egyptian-Israeli peace treaty of March 1979. All these moves, however, were geared mainly to upper-middle-class interests and became increasingly unpopular.

In far less pronounced and dramatic ways, Hafez al-Asad and Saddam Hussein tried to bring a degree of pragmatism into the policies of Syria and Iraq. These attempts were most apparent in the field of foreign rather than domestic affairs. In practice, this emphasis meant that the purist pan-Arabism of Baathist ideology was subordinated to the practical search for useful alliances within the Arab system. However, it never succeeded in overcoming the Syrian-Iraqi split or in providing either country with a durable leadership role in inter-Arab politics. Ultimately, Asad found himself relatively isolated from other Arab countries and forced to develop close relationships with the Soviet Union and the Khomeini regime, while Saddam Hussein became hopelessly bogged down in the costly and pointless war with Iran.

The causes of the problems accompanying the practice of secular nationalism in Turkey, Iran, and the Arab states must be determined and analyzed to provide guidelines for future development. One factor seems to be that in borrowing the idea of nationalism from the West, there was an inadequate understanding in the Middle East that the institution involved more than promoting a new patriotic identity. European nationalism, though its attributes varied in different cases, reached its highest and most durable development in the context of constitutionality and popular sovereignty. In this form, it implicitly asserted that to be viable the integrated national community had to be based on clearly defined limits of power on all levels, an inviolable and consistent system of justice, and the maximum participation of the citizenry in the political process.

In the Middle East, on the contrary, these collateral institutions never really took root, or at least not to an adequate extent. Nationalism was understood rather as a liberation movement aimed at overcoming foreign domination and freeing the indigenous societies from the confining and debilitating influence of traditional Islam, the fetters of an archaic culture, as the Kemalists put it. This very limited and subjective interpretation of nationalism was naïvely viewed as a panacea for all sociopolitical and economic problems, a magic formula that would bring an end to external constraints and establish utopian conditions in the Middle East. Because of its one-dimensional and unsophisticated character, this kind of nationalism was often explained in extravagant rhetorical language, characterized by slogans, generalizations, and oversimplifications.

In many respects, nationalism as it was conceived and practiced in the Middle East resembled the less developed and more radical and transitory forms of the institution that appeared periodically in the West. It contained elements, for example, of the chauvinism encountered in Napoleonic France and Nazi Germany. Although this was not the case everywhere or at all stages, the trend was in this direction. As a result, in many instances Middle Eastern nationalism became closely identified with the ruling elites that sponsored it. A number of regimes were simply examples of the complete monopolization of power by cliques that did not actually represent any genuine national ideals or majority interests. Other less repressive governments introduced various makeshift adjustments to cover up or ameliorate the inadequacies and inequities of their poorly structured or unrepresentative systems.

Except in Turkey, nationalism or the regimes that claimed to represent it had become partially discredited by the 1970s. Though some of the critics and dissenters continued to believe that it was still possible to find yet another revisionist formula to make secular nationalism work in an effective and equitable way, others turned to Marxism or Islam for solutions to the area's increasingly complex problems. Though Marxism had only limited appeal and a relatively small following, the ideas of neofundamentalist Islamic activism acquired a much larger and highly receptive audience. Indeed, the approach of using Islam rather than Westernization as the basis of reform in the Middle East dates back to the eighteenth-century Wahhabi movement in Arabia and other developments of that period.

In countries where opposition to the established government was either restricted or banned altogether, the use of Islam as a vehicle of dissent was appealing because its credentials gave it a degree of immunity from official persecution. All the secular nationalist regimes had either paid lip service to Islam or been extremely careful not to openly challenge it. Islam was, after all, the nominal religion of the vast majority of the area's inhabitants and an integral part of their identity. To most opponents of the existing political order, therefore, association with Islam was the only viable way of expressing and organizing an effective movement of dissent. What ultimately emerged, then, was a remarkable combination of people and ideas. These included completely committed neofundamentalists, individuals who dedicated themselves to Islamic revolution but were either unconsciously or semiconsciously using Islam as a way of altering the status quo, and groups and individuals who had little genuine religious feeling but recognized that the best way to challenge the established order was to associate with Islamic resurgence organizations and to use Islamic symbolism as a practical means of expressing and mobilizing dissent.

The committed neofundamentalists, however, provided the vocabulary and ideology of contemporary Islamic resurgence. It began as an organized movement when Hasan al-Banna founded the Muslim Brotherhood in Egypt in 1928. Initially small and insignificant, the brotherhood grew over the decades and developed an ideology that rejected all the premises of secular nationalism. It also indirectly influenced the emergence of similar organizations in other parts of the Arab world and in Iran.

Though the emphases differ among the neofundamentalist organizations that exist today in the Middle East, they all see the area in a state of chronic disorder and share common positions with regard to the remedy. The contemporary West, representing an immoral culture based on false values, not only conquered the Middle East and took physical control of it but infected the indigenous societies with its own licentious materialism. Among the evils it introduced and nurtured was secular nationalism, a godless cult that rejected Islam and concerned itself solely with the betterment of human communities, which it virtually deified.

The only solution to this deplorable state of affairs, the neofundamentalists maintain, is a comprehensive re-Islamization of the area, a restoration of all the traditional legal, social, and political institutions as originally constituted. At the same time, most or all vestiges of Western culture must be removed, purged from the contaminated societies of the area, by draconian measures if necessary. To accomplish this, the resurgence organizations must repoliticize Islam and proclaim the *jihad* (holy war) as the primary mission and duty of all those participating in the struggle. This message had to be carried to the common people, giving rise to a new Islamic populism that would eventually engulf the Middle East in a powerful movement of reform and renewal. Only then could justice and piety be restored and all forms of foreign intervention, whether political or cultural, be exterminated forever.

This is the basic outlook of Islamic resurgence, the militant form of neofundamentalism that began to have an impact on Middle East politics in the 1970s. It differs from the attitude of the traditionally passive members of the conservative *ulama* (clerical class) in its revolutionary activism. It is at variance with the more circumspect classical fundamentalism of the Wahhabi movement in Saudi Arabia in its radical populism. Though it shares with the Islamic modernist thinkers a belief in reform based on early Islamic models, it is far from them in its pronounced literalism, its lack of any genuinely scholarly approach, and its anti-Western bias, at first qualified and selective but later relatively indiscriminate and prejudiced.

Considering the failings and abuses of secular nationalism in practice, it is not difficult to understand the appeal of contemporary Islamic resurgence. Nevertheless, the movement presents a number of serious problems. First, its often black-and-white view of present circumstances is too simplistic for it to deal with the real world. For example, in no way can the cultural synthesis that has been the byproduct of the modernization process simply be arrested and eradicated. It has been going on in the Middle East for over a century. Furthermore, though certain aspects of Western culture are undeniably unwholesome and disruptive, it is not possible to dismiss the West as a once meritorious civilization now in a degenerate phase, as the Muslim Brotherhood did, or as inherently evil, which has been Khomeini's position. The continuing worth and viability of such Western institutions as constitutionality, popular sovereignty, and equal justice under law have their obvious merits. The notion of a comprehensive Islamic purification of Middle Eastern society and the inauguration of a utopian *umma* in the area— even if not pretending to advocate a return to seventh-century Islam— is therefore naïve and unrealistic.

An even more important shortcoming of resurgence ideology is its one-dimensional understanding of Islam. Because of their preoccupation with repoliticizing Islam and launching a *jihad*, the militants lost sight of the fact that their religion is much more than a doctrine of sociopolitical order. Indeed, most of them are almost ignorant of what historical Islam really was and have little understanding of the remarkable concept of reality developed by the great thinkers of early Islamic civilization. This narrow-mindedness places enormous limitations on their ability to bring a genuinely constructive and helpful message to the admittedly troubled peoples of the Middle East.

Finally, in supporting the use of draconian measures to purify "contaminated" Islamic societies, the neofundamentalists are actually endorsing the highly questionable theory that the end justifies the means. This view fails to take into account the close relationship between means and goals requiring that they remain essentially compatible. The new government in Iran, a creation of neofundamentalist Islam, became enmeshed in this very problem. Though it considered itself the liberator from the tyranny of the shah's regime, its own rule was also authoritarian and involved in violations of human rights.

What is most tragic about these last two points is that they either limit and restrict the development of a correct understanding of Islam or help to discredit Islam altogether. Yet it can be argued that the contemporary Middle East cannot resolve its problems without Islam. This is because Islam is an integral part of Middle Eastern identity and because it has a lot to offer at a time when the world is confronted with complex and seemingly insoluble problems. To put it succinctly, there is no helpful role a one-dimensional interpretation of either secular nationalism or of Islam can play in an area caught in a maze of difficult impasses. The former reduces Islam to a superficial observance, while the latter divests it of its more profound attributes.

It is important to remember that it is seldom possible to find a perfect example of any sociopolitical ideal and that imperfect examples of such ideals are often not completely reprehensible. Not all forms of Islamic neofundamentalism are primarily political in character, and the degrees of intensity differ among the majority that are. Similarly, not all secular and nationalist regimes are devoid of any responsible political philosophy. Some are more liberal and democratic than others.

Nevertheless, it is still possible to make qualified generalizations about Islamic resurgence and secular nationalism in Middle East politics. In significant measure, each has distorted aspects of the tradition it seeks to represent. Though this manipulation may be explained by the exigencies of a society in crisis, it often rendered their attempts to build a more just and viable order illusory and counterproductive. The consequent void in ideological guidelines for reform and reconstruction has left a series of question marks on the political horizon that demands a reexamination of existing doctrines and the introduction of new ideas based on broader and more flexible approaches to Islam and the concept of the nation-state society.

2

The Islamic World View

The term "Islam" is difficult to define because it refers to a tradition with three related yet very distinct dimensions. The interpretive framework developed by Marshall Hodgson is used here, as it is particularly helpful in differentiating the component aspects of that tradition.[1] Islam connotes a religious doctrine based on the belief that Muhammad was the last of the prophetic line that began with Abraham and that the Quran is the final and complete form of the earlier revealed scriptures known as the Old and New Testaments. These beliefs became the foundation of a system of devotional observances associated with the practice of Islam as a religion.

Islamdom refers to the historical society of Muslims that after the inaugural phase constituted an imperial polity. In this sense, it was a political community, though at later stages many often rivalistic Islamic states came into existence. Islamdom, in turn, produced what Hodgson dubbed the "Islamicate," an eclectic culture and a pattern of social interaction. These dimensions of the Islamic heritage differ not only in character but in durability. Whereas Islam as religious practice has remained virtually the same since its inception, Islamdom as a political order was unstable and transitory, and the Islamicate as a cultural tradition changed in emphasis from one era to the next without losing a certain continuity of the whole.

A brief survey follows of those aspects of the Islamic tradition relevant to the present study. There are obvious difficulties entailed in making broad generalizations about a subject as vast and diversified as Islamic civilization. Yet it is possible to identify certain recurrent themes in Islamicate culture and sociopolitical orientation and to draw conclusions about them. The treatment here is designed to illustrate some significant relationships between what the Muslims of former times did and thought and the ways in which contemporary Muslims in the Middle East are trying to deal with the problems of modernization without relinquishing their Islamic identity. This survey is not intended to be an overview of

Islamic history but a statement about the connection between the past and the present. More specifically, it is concerned with analyzing the interpretive understanding of the Islamic heritage that the Muslims of the modern Middle East developed in the course of bringing Islamic themes into the political process.

The Humanist Theme

Though humanism is sometimes associated with profane or secular philosophies, it is also an important dimension of most religions. Humanism is not only a doctrine and way of life centered on human interests but on human values as well. It involves the quest for moral guidelines and a way of dealing with the problems of transgression and laxity. In this respect, it seeks to create symbols that explain the nature of true man and dehumanized man.

The Islamic tradition is replete with images of man as upright and degenerate. It is deeply concerned with the question of order and disorder, both in the individual and in society. The line of prophets from Abraham to Muhammad represents the search for moral order as revealed by God, and Muhammad himself provides the model of the ideal man. Similarly, the first *umma*, composed of the Prophet, his Companions, and the converts of Medina, is the example of the virtuous community. The recalcitrant Meccans reflect the other side of the dichotomy—the idolatrous society bent on protecting its corrupt religious practices and its lucrative business interests to the point that it was completely unwilling to accept Muhammad's message.

The war between Medina and Mecca during the Prophet's lifetime was the first image of the *jihad*, the struggle against the ungodly that was to be the historical mission of Islam. The intended premise surrounding the entire episode is that the Islamic way of life is incompatible with that of unbelieving mundane societies. The two are by definition in a state of war with each other because they are diametrically opposed. From the Islamic point of view, however, the conflict between *dar al-Islam* (realm of Islam) and *dar al-harb* (realm of war) is not conducted by the Muslims for glory or booty or revenge but to spread Islam in the world. The *umma* seeks to enlighten its adversaries, though it cannot compromise with them. Ideally, victory should be followed by the conversion of the vanquished. Conquered monotheists who chose to remain Christian, Jewish, or Zoroastrian could do so, but as *dhimmis* (protected subjects) with lower status and higher tax responsibilities. The few who rejected any monotheistic commitment were either enslaved or executed.

Underlying this early picture of the Islamic world view is a message concerning man's spiritual dimension. The ideal human condition is one of harmony with God, achieved by submission to his will and the conduct of relationships with others in conformity with the virtues of brotherhood (*ukhwa*) and mercy (*rahma*). This is, at least, the theoretical position, whether Muslims actually practiced it or not. Islam is not other-worldly and disinterested in what goes on in the earthly realm. It is deeply concerned with human behavior and with the historical process. What people do reflects their spiritual depth, the inner life that is the link between man and God.

Muhammad is the model of the perfectly balanced man—deeply spiritual yet active in the world as teacher and leader at the same time. Muslims look to him as an example and derive their sense of unity and brotherhood through him. The communal Friday prayer is a manifestation of this combination of spirituality and fraternity, for here the worship of God and the love of men for each other come together. The same occurs during the annual pilgrimage to Mecca.

Unquestionably, Muslims historically fell short of realizing these Islamic ideals. During some periods they were closer to them than in others. The multidimensional character of Islam as originally founded by the Prophet, however, did lead to a highly refined and diversified civilization under the Umayyad and Abbasid empires. The Muslims of this earlier age may not have been more pious or spiritually oriented than at other times. Yet the intellectuals among them did produce an extremely rich culture based on a synthesis of Islamic and non-Islamic ideas and traditions. Perhaps their most profound achievement was their understanding of the harmonious interrelationship between man and nature, a picture of a universal structure seldom equaled in other times and places.

To arrive at a comparative analysis of contemporary Islamic resurgence, it is important to consider the accomplishments of Islam's classical age. Because it was in all respects multifaceted, it is best referred to as the Islamic synthesis.

The Islamic Synthesis

When Islam erupted out of its original Arabian setting and forged a sprawling Middle Eastern empire, it developed other dimensions that made it a ramified and eclectic culture of the highest quality. The conquered territories included the former Byzantine provinces in the Fertile Crescent and North Africa, Persia, Afghanistan, lower Turkistan, parts of the Indian subcontinent, and eventually Spain. Most of these areas were endowed with a high level of civilization, notably that of

Byzantium and Persia. They were also largely Christian or Zoroastrian. The Arab attitude toward the cultures of the vanquished peoples was open and receptive, facilitating a far-reaching cultural exchange.

Initially, the imperial policy was to set up a ruling Arab warrior caste in the newly acquired provinces, while keeping the existing bureaucracies intact. Though conversion was not forced on *dhimmis,* many were induced to adopt Islam because of the preferential tax obligations of Muslims. The non-Arabs who did convert to Islam became known as the *mawali,* and among their grievances was the disinclination of the governing class either to adjust their tax status or to treat them as equals.

With the accession to power of the Abbasids in A.D. 750 the phase of Arab domination came to an end. The officially sponsored movement of peoples (*shuubiyya*) was a de-Arabizing and cosmopolitanizing step that accelerated the cultural blending initiated by the Umayyads. Though the caliph continued to be an Arab, the *mawali* were fully instated and began to play an active role in government and cultural affairs. They were an important element in the Islamic synthesis that began to flower at this stage.

As already noted, even during the Arab-oriented Umayyad period the Arabs had no hostility toward the peoples and cultures of the conquered lands. On the contrary, they took an interest in the advanced civilizations of the subject populations. Following the Abbasid succession, many facets of these alien cultures were brought within a religious framework and made part of the developing Islamicate culture and civilization.

If a literal interpretation of Islam had been predominant at this time, the celebrated achievements of the classical period would never have been possible. In the field of architecture, for example, it was known that the Prophet had criticized one of his wives for making an addition to their dwelling in his absence. He objected because he regarded preoccupation with such matters as a waste of time—certainly far less worthwhile than pursuing one's religious vocation. But since he had never directly condemned construction, an elaborate architectural tradition developed during the Umayyad Caliphate and flourished under the Abbasids and other dynasties. The exquisite design and decoration of the great early mosques represent the incorporation of Byzantine and Persian style within an Islamic framework. This bringing together of Muslim and foreign traditions gave Islamic civilization its resiliency and high level of refinement.

The development of Islamic philosophy would also have been precluded by an enforced literalism. The conservative school of thought insisted that God and the unfolding of providence were beyond human comprehension and that it was blasphemous to place God within the interpretive limits of man's rationality. Yet a philosophical tradition did arise in the early Abbasid period and had official sanction until the mid-ninth century A.D. Without it Islam could not have reached the advanced understanding of reality that took Islamic theology and perception of the world far beyond the state of textual exegesis.

The neo-Platonism of al-Kindi, al-Farabi, and Ibn Sina were criticized for their pronounced intellectualism. Yet it would have been difficult to expand the concept of divine unity (*tawhid*) into a sophisticated picture of universal relationships without their insights. This concept was extremely important in classical Islamic civilization and pervades all aspects of its advanced culture. The beautiful floral designs in many of the great mosques, for example, symbolize the interwoven matrix of nature, always reaching upward toward the divine source of existence. Flowing water in the decorative canals found in some mosque courtyards represents purification, tranquility, and the movement of streams and rivers toward the sea, of all things toward a common goal. The constant theme is the dependence of everything in the world on the creator God and the inevitable links among the elements of nature that this universal condition implies.

The delicacy of Islamic art and architecture and the profundity of Islamic philosophy enriched Islam and the civilization of the classical period. They form an important part of a legacy that helped to preserve and build one of the world's great religious cultures. It was derived, however, from the Islamic synthesis, the process by which Muslims incorporated the best of other traditions within their own, broadening rather than diluting the Islamic focus. Islam as a civilization is consequently eclectic, just as Islam as a religion is universal. These two attributes are inseparable aspects of the same heritage. The combination is the source of its vitality, its inner strength.

An unfortunate development in the cultural history of Islam was the closing of the doors of *ijtihad*, originally thought by scholars to have taken place at the end of the ninth century A.D. but now considered by some to have happened in the sixteenth.[2] It seems evident, however, that *ijtihad* was either restricted or less frequently used beginning with the earlier time. This decreased use was partly because a certain tension was created by the constant attempt to preserve a reliable orthodoxy against the threat of innovation (*bida*) posed by the eclectic origins of Islamic civilization, though the achievement of incorporating external elements without allowing them to dominate had been remarkable.[3] Islam has always preserved a delicate balance between the extremes of cosmopolitanism on the one hand and the danger of becoming parochial on the other. Yet the need to restrict the continuation of free inquiry reflected a fear that further elaboration of the tradition might be dangerous. Perhaps, however, this restriction did not stem so much from the line of cultural development, which had been outstanding indeed, as from the political dimension of Islam, which was far more problematical.

The Political Dimension

Islam has had a political dimension from the beginning. When Muhammad emigrated from Mecca with his companions and became head of the first *umma* in Medina, he assumed a political as well as religious role. He was both the spiritual leader and ruler of a theocratic community.

Inasmuch as the *umma* was charged with the sanctification of its own members and with the historic mission of spreading the Quran in a hostile world, it was always assumed that the Muslims constituted a political body dedicated to a religious goal. There could never be a division between church and state because the believers were agents of a divine process unfolding in the mundane world. After the death of the Prophet, a line of caliphs (successors) took his place as religious and political leaders of the *umma*, preserving the purity of the Muslims and leading them in their missionary vocation.

This image of the Islamic state is highly idealized and has utopian overtones. The picture is one of a harmonious community, united by its brotherly spirit and its dedication to the practice and spreading of Islam. The Prophet was a model ruler, pious and just, courageous and wise. These conditions prevailed while Muhammad was alive, and they were expected to continue under the supervision of the caliphs after his death. But this turned out to be a serious miscalculation.

The central theme in Islamic political doctrine as originally conceived is the idea of the unity of the *umma*. Factionalism and other forms of division were thought to be highly disruptive to the proper functioning of the Islamic community. It could not preserve its own pious order or accomplish its missionary role if discord developed in its ranks. The whole theory of the *umma* rests on the premise that it remain united. Without cohesiveness, its religous vocation would be undermined.

This aspect of the Islamic world view eventually created some discrepancies between theory and reality that had to be resolved through a revision of philosophical perspectives. The idealized images of the caliph and the *umma* developed in the inaugural period placed some impediments on the ability to consider ways of counteracting special interests, which play a role in any political situation. Despite changes in the theory of the Islamic state, therefore, there were no adequate safeguards against the emergence of divisiveness within the *umma*, a diminution of the solidarity everyone took for granted.

Political factionalism appeared very early in Islamic history, within a few years of the Prophet's death. The source of conflict was the question of succession to the caliphate, for which no procedural guidelines had been laid down. Though Abu Bakr and Umar served as the first two caliphs without opposition, rival camps developed with the accession of Uthman in A.D. 644. The powerful Umayyad clan, to which the new caliph belonged, wanted to establish a hereditary dynastic claim. This approach was challenged by the supporters of the Prophet's first cousin and son-in-law, Ali, and his blood line as rightful heirs to the caliphate. Yet another aspiring group was led by Muhammad's last wife, Aisha, and her colleagues.

The first armed encounter was between Aisha and the Alids in A.D. 656. Though Ali was victorious and became the fourth caliph, the Umayyads established their own dynastic rule after his assassination in A.D. 661 by a member of the dissident Kharijite sect, which insisted that succession to the caliphate be determined by the free choice of the whole community of believers. This event was the beginning of a prolonged struggle between the Umayyad Caliphate and the party of Ali (Shiat Ali), or Shiites. The Shiites became a separate sect within Islam following the death of Ali's son, Hussein, in the Battle of Karbala in A.D. 681. This permanent and far more serious division among the Muslims virtually destroyed the myth of the united *umma*, though the majority Sunnis continued to endorse the theory.

The Umayyads became involved in further armed conflict over the caliphate in a war against Meccan claimants just a few years after the Battle of Karbala. Though they successfully contained this threat to their authority, however, they faced increasing opposition from various dissident groups within the now extensive empire. These included undisciplined Arab tribal elements, the disaffected *mawali*, the *ulama* who took issue with the secular tendencies of the Umayyads, and the rebellious Shiites. Ultimately, these forces of discontent became unmanageable. The Abbasid family, part of the Prophet's own Hashemite clan and now situated in southern Mesopotamia, was able to coordinate a revolutionary movement against the Umayyads and to found a successor caliphate in A.D. 749–750.

Resplendent in their new capital at Baghdad, the Abbasid caliphs sought to inaugurate an era of reconciliation that would counteract the divisive trends that had beset Islam and to reaffirm the unity of the Muslims. Though they were initially successful in creating a spirit of solidarity, they eventually had to contend with regional separatist movements not infrequently associated with Shiite sectarianism. This problem became increasingly formidable and gradually led to the fragmentation of the empire. Indeed, after the Shiite Buwayhid emirs from Iran took over the running of temporal affairs in Baghdad in A.D. 945, the authority of the Abbasid caliphs was largely nominal and symbolic.

In the context of these untoward developments in early Islamic history, several problems arose concerning political practice and tradition. Because the idealized picture of the caliph, the *umma*, and the *sharia* (Islamic law) became an integral part of the Islamic self-image, the question of the use and misuse of power was never adequately analyzed. The assumption that an honorable ruler presiding over a dedicated community through a divinely ordained legal system would fulfill the mission of Islam was bound to be challenged when applied to the dynamics of power politics in a far from perfect world. This was certainly the case in early Islamic history. Despite the theory of what the caliph was supposed to be, only a few of those occupying the post were exceptional. Some were impetuous, and most tried to keep a tight monopoly on power. Though in principle the caliph was bound by the *sharia*, the actual subordination of the judiciary to the executive meant that in practice the ruler could do virtually whatever he wanted.[4] A recent study, however, reveals that during the Umayyad and Abbasid periods, "religious communities developed independently of the states or empires that ruled them. The *'ulema* regulated local communal and religious life by serving as judges, administrators, teachers, and religious advisers to Muslims."[5] Despite this de facto separation of religion and state on the administrative level, however, actual political power was exercised by the ruling institution.

A closely related problem was that, except in matters related to property, Islamic law places greater emphasis on duties and obligations than on personal rights and prerogatives.[6] The Quran upholds certain principles, including the dignity of mankind, racial equality, the close relationship between men and women, religious freedom, and the protection of people from degradation and want.[7] But these do not constitute a legally binding bill of rights or an adequate safeguard against political abuse. This combination of a weak judiciary, the lack of constitutional constraints on the exercise of power, and an undefined code of individual rights engendered a political system in which misrule and injustice were relatively common and decisions of established regimes were often arbitrary and based on personal connections and favoritism.

The outstanding political theoreticians dealt with the problem of a discrepancy between the ideal of Islamic order and the reality of what it had become by accepting a de facto separation of *din* (religion) and *dawla* (state). They insisted on obedience to established authorities, even if they were unjust, to preserve the unity of the *umma*.[8] As Ibn Jamaa put it, the most important thing was that the Muslims "speak with one voice."[9] This position, however, was not based on cynicism or pure expediency but on the desire to differentiate between the established imperfections of Islamdom as a political community in historical time and the eternal validity of Islam as the key to redemption in eschatological time. The realism of this interpretation notwithstanding, the contradiction between the idealism of the original Muslim world view and the standard political behavior that evolved in the practical realm left Islam without an adequate system of precedents to establish and preserve a tradition of stable political continuity.

The termination of the Abbasid Caliphate in 1258 was eventually followed by the formation of the Ottoman Empire, which revived the military power of Islamdom in the Middle East. But the new imperium also became the victim of divisive forces, though a certain resiliency was maintained for centuries. Furthermore, it perpetuated the tradition of a dominant executive authority, despite its accomplishments in political decentralization. In the history of Islam as a state system, unity and justice often remained unfulfilled ideals. On the urban level, however, the *ulama* managed in some cases to preserve intercommunal bonds and a reasonable degree of administrative equity, at least among the established interest groups.[10] In any event, the remarkable achievements in the cultural sphere were never matched in the field of politics. It can therefore be said that although Islam always had a political dimension, in this very area it has been weakest in practice.

The eclipse of the Ottoman system set in when its own institutions became dysfunctional and the external challenges confronting it required greater flexibility than is possible in a traditional authoritarian polity. The attempts at reform were always inadequate, as separatist movements gradually diminished the geographic scope of the empire and foreign intrusion increasingly restricted its sovereignty. Nationalism, first in the Balkans and later in the Arab provinces, led to fragmentation, while the European powers established ever tighter controls over Ottoman territories.

In the nineteenth century, the European intrusion initially took the form of imposed settlements, such as the resolution of the Greek insurrection of the 1820s, of Muhammad Ali's conquest of Syria in the 1830s, of the civil war in Lebanon in 1860, and of the Balkan crisis in the 1870s. Later, the Europeans engaged in outright partition of various parts of the empire. Britain acquired control of Cyprus in 1878 and of Egypt in 1882, having already established dominance over the Arab sheikhdoms in the Gulf region and South Arabia. In 1907, Iran and Afghanistan, which had been the object of imperialist manipulation for a century, were divided into zones of foreign influence by Great Britain and Russia, virtually terminating their already considerably eroded independence. France had conquered Algeria in 1830 and extended its control over North Africa to include Tunisia in 1881 and Morocco in 1912. Libya became an Italian colony in 1911. The Fertile Crescent provinces, which had remained part of the Ottoman Empire, were reorganized and placed under British and French mandatory administrations after World War I. Turkey proper was defeated in the war and much of it was to be parceled out to France, Italy, Great Britain, the Armenians, and the Kurds, though this was prevented by the Turkish resistance under Atatürk's leadership. By 1918, then, the entire Middle East, with the exception of Yemen and central Arabia, had been partitioned into zones of foreign occupation or influence.

Looked at from a twentieth-century perspective, the Islamic political tradition in the Middle East, having precariously survived many centuries of vicissitude, came to an end with the dissolution of the Ottoman Empire. Except in the traditionalist Arabian states, political systems were secularized throughout the area under the banner of nationalism. The Ottoman caliphate was dismantled, and many aspects of institutional life were de-Islamized. The strong trend toward Westernization, with its emphasis on utilitarian values, precluded the retention of Islam's political dimension as the basis of law and public affairs. Indeed, many had unfavorable memories of the traditional order and had even actively opposed it. The preference now was for Islam as personal "experience," as it was put in the early years of Kemalist Turkey, or for the elimination of Islam as a significant force in social life.

The eradication of Islamic sociopolitical institutions was a momentous and unprecedented development. The ultimate consequences and the ramifications of the extensive changes it would inevitably entail were the subject of intense controversy at the time the transition took place. But the secularists did not really foresee the repercussions that might ensue from the changes they had introduced. They generally assumed that the new nationalist order would be successful in meeting the challenges of the post-Ottoman era and that in any event the political dimension of Islam was no longer relevant. Virtually none of them stopped to consider what would happen if nationalism failed to achieve a successful reconstruction of public order in the Middle East. The unposed and unanswered questions on this subject were like ghosts that were destined to haunt future generations of the secular age.

Historical and Psychological Legacies

Muslims in the contemporary Middle East have inherited certain legacies from their Islamic past. It is important to determine exactly what these are because the area's people are currently searching for alternatives to institutional and behavioral models derived largely from the West. Unfortunately, the tendency among those disenchanted with secular nationalism in practice is to turn to popularized forms of Islamic resurgence without examining or analyzing their implications and relative legitimacy. This often impulsive recourse to Islam is reminiscent of the earlier fascination with nationalism, which was embraced without enough thoughtful consideration and assumed to be an emancipating panacea. Lacking in both cases was the realization that any major change in sociopolitical and cultural orientation involves a variety of choices within the broader outlines of the alternative itself. This kind of political shortsightedness was, nevertheless, an understandable product of the traumatic experiences of foreign intrusion and domestic innovation that had severely destabilized Middle Eastern society.

As noted earlier, Islam is multifaceted and based on the combination of a richly endowed religious culture and a comprehensive sociopolitical theory and system. Though its most notable and valuable achievements have been in the cultural field, this aspect of the tradition has had a relatively dormant history for many centuries and has not really undergone a revival in modern times. What is most tragic about this is that the humanism, eclecticism, and profound understanding of nature and the existential interrelatedness of things, which are found in classical Islamic phenomenology, would be particularly helpful to Muslims as they attempt to cope with many contemporary problems. In a world caught up in a maze of material conflicts, contrived sloganism, and deliberately falsified images, soundness of metaphysical perspective is ultimately the most desperately needed antidote. This applies to all contemporary cultures, including that of the West. If and when Muslims come to realize this, they may be able to recover an especially useful and rewarding part of their own legacy.

As it is, the recent Islamic revival has focused on the political dimension, with all its concomitant shortcomings and psychological problems. Many of the restraints that surrounded politics in traditional Islamic societies have reappeared in the contemporary reconstruction. The utopianism of the dedicated *umma* and pious leadership concepts have been reconstructed in a more intense form by the resurgence movement. The underlying reality is, of course, different. In the modern version it comprises the embittered and angry crowd demonstrating its unbridled hostility in the streets, orchestrated by the rhetoric of a charismatic religious leader using a doctrine of purification as a political tool. Democracy is ridiculed as an alien concept, permitting the unimpeded practice of authoritarian rule. This is made easier by the lack of an adequate bill of rights or system of checks and balances in Islamic political theory, as well as by the idea that draconian measures are required to counteract the infection of Middle Eastern society by degenerate foreign cultural influences.

Discrepancies between theory and reality were dealt with in traditional Islamic societies by philosophical reformulations and practical measures taken by the *ulama*. In the contemporary Middle East, however, virtually all political groups do not even acknowledge that such a contradiction exists. The religious dedication of those in or led by modern resurgence movements is an expression of the reoriented and redirected anger of abused, disaffected, and disillusioned elements in respective countries of the area. The desire to address grievances underlies the interest in the sanctification of Islamic communities. In Iran, where a neofundamentalist "Islamic Republic" has been established, the myth of the reformed and unified *umma* is propagated, despite the deep political, ethnic, and regional divisions. Also in Iran, the widely disseminated images of the pious leader and an emancipating Islamic regime conceal the adroit consolidation of power and repression of the opposition that mark the real attributes of the political situation.

The Islamic premise that with the completion of revelation in the form of the Quran the *umma* was charged with the responsibility of spreading God's truth in the world generated a complex psychological syndrome. In effect, a human community was asked to perform a superhuman task. This premise, in turn, led to the belief in the dedicated character of the caliph and the *umma*. When this failed to materialize in practice and the mission remained only partially fulfilled, a sense of partial failure was generated on at least an unconscious level. The standard way of dealing with this failure in former times was to preserve a facade of proper order even though the reality was far from the theoretical ideal. This approach was generally accepted by most people, however, either because it made them feel more comfortable about the shortcomings of the Islamic state or because they had reconciled themselves to the imperfections of Islam as a political system and found compensation in religious practice and the efforts of the *ulama* to maintain a degree of administrative equity.

The same situation prevails in the contemporary Middle East, though the ways of addressing it are less mature. In Iran, the one place where militant neofundamentalist Islam can be examined as a regime in power, an elaborate version of the utopian myth has been developed to hide the failures and abuses of the resurgence approach to Islamic revival. The same cult of the personality in leadership and injustice in political practice, which the Iranian regime criticizes in nationalist states of the area, are prominent in the very system over which it presides. This kind of hyopcrisy reflects the highly disturbed nature of political psy-

chology in the contemporary Middle East and the limited grasp the
neofundamentalists have of the spiritual and humanist dimensions of
Islamicate culture.

The sweeping generalizations about everything, the highly literalist
interpretation of Islam, and the demagogic political style that characterize
most contemporary Islamic resurgence movements have seriously impeded
the quest of many Muslims for a religious revival that genuinely addresses
modern problems. These attributes are intellectually crippling and preclude the rediscovery of those Islamic traditions that could be most
helpful today. Certainly, there is no possibility of recovering any of the
profound metaphysical conceptualism of classical Islam in a totalitarian
system that prohibits free thought, severely restricts the behavior and
movements of the entire population, and rejects most forms of dissent
or the expression of views on Islam that differ from the official ideology.
Though this kind of authoritarianism may not be envisioned in some
neofundamentalist ideologies[11] or advocated by all Islamic resurgence
groups, it was adopted by the militants in the one case where they
came to power.

The leaders and followers of the contemporary Islamic resurgence
movements in the Middle East think they are restoring Islam and rescuing
the peoples of the area from the contamination of Western culture. More
accurately, however, they are reviving the psychological syndrome that
was so troublesome in earlier centuries. Many of the Sunni activists
cite the fourteenth-century political theorist, Ibn Taymiyya, to justify
their revolt against established "illegitimate" rule.[12] Yet their own doctrines
implicitly preclude the rights of dissent within the type of sociopolitical
system they are trying to establish. Once in power, they could easily
become involved in the traditional pattern of coercion, repression, and
falsification, violating the most basic human rights behind a facade of
piety and purification. At least the example of Shiite Iran strongly
suggests this. And though Shiite Islam differs from Sunni thought and
practice, the orientation and ideology of contemporary neofundamentalism are very much the same in both cases.

The tendency to dismiss much that is of Western origin, which is
common among most but not all resurgence groups and ideologies, is
on the surface a rejection of the materialistic and permissive aspects of
Western culture. But it is more significantly a defense against the
challenges that would be brought to bear on neofundamentalism's narrow
interpretation of Islam and the modern world by Western techniques
of analysis and assessment. Admitting foreign elements into a literalist
Islamic system would also advance the idea of a new Islamic eclecticism
and favor the revival of Islam's cultural as opposed to political legacy.
The neofundamentalist emphasis on the desecularization of Middle

Eastern society and the repoliticization of Islam often reaches the point of suggesting that the religion is primarily political. There is undoubtedly an unconscious fear that a broader interpetation would encourage re-suscitation of the cultural tradition, which was distinctly synthetic and implicitly opposed to the subordination of humanistic pursuits to the requirements of Islam as a political order, especially when absolutist in character.

In opting for an Islamic reconstruction that placed almost total emphasis on building a utopian political order, the militant neofunda-mentalist movement inherited the least useful and most problematical legacy of Islam from the past. Though opposed to the monopolization of power practiced by nationalist regimes, most resurgence ideologies can rather easily be used to justify an authoritarian form of Islamic government. Given the declining level of tolerance for political manip-ulation and extravagant slogans in today's Middle East, this kind of Islamic revival has built-in obstacles to its own success. Indeed, its main opportunity to come to power or exercise any significant influence is to play on the emotions of the disaffected and ignorant masses. Should they ever take over in this way, however, they would still have to cope with the ever larger educated segment of the population, not to mention the majority that feel a deep need for some kind of genuine democracy.

The most unfortunate aspect of the neofundamentalist movement is its inherently hostile attitude toward a revival of Islam's cultural legacies in the intellectual field and toward constructive use of the best in the Western tradition. As mentioned earlier, the nonpolitical dimensions of Islam can and should play a useful role in the search for effective ways of dealing with contemporary problems. If neofundamentalism blocks the recovery of Islamic humanism and metaphysics or discredits the idea of using any part of the Islamicate cultural heritage in developing modern sociopolitical life, it will have destroyed an important option open to the peoples of the Middle East. Similarly, if it prevents the synthesis of Western and Islamic intellectual traditions, which formed the basis of Islam's greatest earlier achievements, it will have created a barrier to the development of human resources in all areas of endeavor. Within the context of these realities the Islamic question in Middle East politics is currently being posed. There are crucial choices to be made, and the ultimate character of the future is at stake. The right choices depend, however, on the degree to which the consequences of each decision are fully and maturely understood.

3

The Secular Nationalist Response

The ideology of nationalism, which spread throughout much of the Middle East in the first quarter of the twentieth century, derived its force and popularity from the moribund state of the traditional polities in the area and the void in viable alternative doctrines of sociopolitical reconstruction. It was also appealing because of its apparent utility and promise of a more equitable system of government. Yet Middle Eastern nationalism emphasized patriotism and liberation but was relatively weak in its development of the constitutional political concepts that had made most forms of European nationalism both viable and lasting. In this respect, it differed from many of the Western models it was trying to imitate. In the American revolutionary movement, for example, the quest for independence was inseparably tied to the highly sophisticated political ideals and programs of the founding fathers. In the Middle East, in contrast, most of the national liberation movements were accompanied by a less clearly conceived picture of the anticipated future order. This feature left them vulnerable to diversity of interpretation and the manipulation of power elites.

Turkey

The components of Turkish nationalism, first systematically developed by Ziya Gökalp (1876–1924), are perhaps closest to the Western tradition in that they combine a form of democratic populism with the concept of Turkish national identity. But Gökalp's thought was mainly focused on redefining the Turkish cultural ethos on the basis of a presumed affiliation with Western civilization.[1]

He was never a practicing politician or a political theorist, though he did play a role in drafting the Turkish constitution of 1924. Strongly influenced by the new science of sociology, particularly the writings of Emile Durkheim, he elaborated a theory of the relationship between culture and civilization that held that a Mediterranean-centered civilizational entity, commonly referred to as "Western," contained several national cultures, including that of the Turks. Hence, the Turks, as well as other eastern and southern Mediterranean peoples, were just as Western as the Europeans. The only difference was that their kind of monotheism was Islamic rather than Christian, and their language Turkish rather than German, French, or Italian.

Though based on broad generalizations and inadequately explored or analyzed assumptions, Gökalp's doctrine of "Turkism," as he called it, greatly facilitated the transition from Ottoman orientation to Turkish nationalism among the Anatolian Turks. Gökalp performed an important service for his people in defining a new concept of national identity to which they could relate at a time when the Ottoman Empire was being replaced by states representing its component nationalities. He provided the ideological guidelines for an escape from the Islamic institutional framework of Ottomanism to a modern Western way of life based on popular culture. This was because his central theme was the resuscitation of a Turkish national ethos.

This contribution aside, Gökalp's Turkism does not include a political philosophy of any profundity. Except for an assumption that Turkish folk culture was inherently democratic, it fails to probe deeply into such intricate questions as constitutionality, representation, and human rights. Gökalp did emphasize freedom of press but primarily because he considered it essential to the indoctrination process through which Turks would reorient themselves in the new nationalist ideology. Though Gökalp certainly anticipated a liberal democratic Turkish republic, his own doctrine provided no safeguards against the appearance of more restrictive polities in the emerging nation.

Gökalp felt that Islam had a role to play in the future national life of the Turks but in terms of religion as the basis of personal spirituality and the transmission of eternal values. He favored the separation of institutional Islam from government, that is, its depoliticization. In these respects, he laid the foundation of the Kemalist state's approach to Islam, though he was more religious than Mustafa Kemal. The main problem with the Turkist attitude toward Islam is that it reduced this formerly dominant theme in Middle Eastern sociopolitical life to a mere facet of Turkish national culture in a rapid and sweeping manner that left no time to consider the ultimate implications and consequences of such a momentous step. Although there was not necessarily anything negative in the attempt to look at Islam from a different perspective, the advisability of subordinating Islam to the cult of nationalism without a comparative analysis of the relationship of each system to matters of ultimate importance is questionable.

In any event, with the end of the war in 1918 and the success of the Turkish resistance movement under Mustafa Kemal, a new Turkish nation based on Gökalp's doctrine of Turkism was launched in the early 1920s and achieved international recognition in 1923. There was a confrontation between the Kemalist secularists and the Islamists over the institutional character of the state. With the Grand National Assembly's abolition of the sultanate on November 1, 1922, and of the caliphate on March 3, 1924, however, the comprehensive secularization of Turkey became a matter of course.

The Kemalist government systematically dismantled Islam as the institutional basis of Turkish life in the 1920s and 1930s. Islamic law was replaced by civil codes, and education was secularized and placed under the authority of a new Ministry of Education. The constitution of 1928 omitted any mention of Islam as the religion of the Turkish state, and the former royal family was banished. Traditional dress was legally abolished in 1925, polygamy was prohibited in 1926, and Latin script replaced Arabic for the writing of the Turkish language in 1928. The political emancipation of women, including the right to vote and hold public office, was legally enacted in 1934, and the Western weekend was adopted in 1935.

Though no attempt was made to obstruct the purely devotional practice of Islam, Mustafa Kemal and others in charge of the reconstruction of Turkey as a modern secular nation deliberately sought to propagate a different understanding of Islam, one that would be more compatible with the new sociopolitical order.[2] All religious matters came under the supervision of a Board of Religious Affairs and a Board of Pious Foundations. The aim of these organizations was to foster the idea of a "natural Islam," which emphasized religious "experience" as opposed to Islam as an institutionalized sociopolitical system. This initiative sought to revive the more profound spiritual aspects of Islam in place of the previously dominant political dimension. Yet it was also part of a broader program of indoctrination designed to alter radically the perceptions, beliefs, and loyalties of the Turkish people.

Mustafa Kemal, himself hardly more than a nominal Muslim, regarded Islam as a cohesive force at best.[3] It could be useful as one of several identity symbols capable of promoting a common national ideal among the Turks. This subordination of Islam to the interests of the secular nationalist state was a basic tenet of Kemalism, and opposition to it was not tolerated. Said Nursi, who had sided with Mustafa Kemal during the struggle for independence, later took issue with the secularization and Westernization of the country.[4] Nursi wanted the new Turkey to be an Islamic state based on the *sharia* and ruled by a council of *ulama*.

Though he did gather a following, he was often imprisoned and exiled for his political activities.

This kind of intolerance for dissent from Kemalism became an integral part of the new political order in nationalist Turkey. Though less pronounced than the conformism enforced by other secular regimes in the Middle East, it nevertheless represented a narrower approach to nationalism than is generally found in the West. Lacking the necessary political and legal safeguards to ensure adequate restraints on the exercise of power, it became susceptible to a resort to extraconstitutional procedures. The crisis of 1960, the destabilization of the political system, the frequent interventions of the military to restore order and protect the principles of Kemalism, and the dominant role played by the army since 1980 are all symptomatic of an underlying weakness in the doctrine of Turkish nationalism as formulated and implemented. In Turkey, the problem may have involved less inequities and violations of civil rights than in other parts of the Middle East, but it remains a reflection of the broader political issue currently surfacing throughout the area.

Another issue raised by the intense secularization of Turkey was a certain psychological void created by the disappearance of Islam from many facets of daily life. As philosophy professor Mehmet Emin succinctly put it: "How can we strengthen in the souls [of the people] beliefs *useful* to society? Can Islam, reshaped to fit the requirements of secular life, satisfy this need of the people [for spiritual fulfillment]?"[5] Under the nationalist order, the measure of all things was utility, and since Islam was regarded as having little utilitarian value, it was discarded from public life. But Islam historically is more than a doctrine, more than private belief and worship. It is also a culture and an institutional framework governing all aspects of interpersonal relations. The question that has to be asked is whether pure utilitarianism can satisfy all needs in a society that considers itself in some respects Islamic. There is also the added problem presented by the division of Turkey into a secularized urban class and a still rather traditional rural populace.

Iran

Iranian nationalism developed gradually in the context of popular movements aimed at political liberalization and the eradication of foreign controls. The intense Anglo-Russian political involvement in Iran throughout the nineteenth century, coupled with massive economic penetration beginning in 1872, became a major internal issue in the early 1900s. The ruling Qajar dynasty's acquiescence to this intrusion by the British and Russian empires led to demands for reform by the urban middle classes and the mullahs (clergy). The first demonstrations at the end of

1904 continued through the following year and took the form of a powerful constitutional movement in 1906. By summer, the shah was forced to promulgate a constitution based on the Western model and establishing a popularly elected representative assembly, or *majlis*.

This protest, though primarily concerned with the liberalization of the political process and the extrication of the country from the inordinate degree of great power influence, was also an early expression of an emerging Iranian nationalism.[6] The constitution represented a specific Iranian nation, or *millat-i Iran*, and the *majlis* was supposed to be the voice of its sovereign people. There was, however, no clearly defined or systematically developed ideology of Iranian nationalism. This was because Iran was, in fact, a multinational country with a dominant Persian population, as well as Kurds, Arabs, Baluchis, Turks, and Turkomen. The nationalism first expressed at this time was really Persian nationalism parading as a broader Iranian movement. Though the non-Persian nationalities may have shared the common opposition to foreign intervention and domestic misrule, the new political order kept Shiite Islam as the religion of the state and Persian as the official language. The pluralistic character of Iranian society precluded an ethnic interpretation of nationalism. Yet the 1906 revolution implicitly combined a distinctly Persian nationalism and a program of reform. Ideological precepts were never developed because such a formulation would risk alienating the other national entities in Iran on the nationalist issue and the ruling dynasty and other political elites on the question of the ultimate direction of constitutional reform.

The uncertainties and ambiguities surrounding this initial liberal nationalist movement in Iran persisted throughout the country's subsequent political development. The constitutional system launched in 1906 lasted only until the end of 1911, when Russian pressure backed up by military intervention forced the closing of the *majlis*. This event confirmed the structure of external control initiated by the partition arrangement of the 1907 Anglo-Russian Agreement. Iran then entered a period of political retrogression, devoid of responsible leadership and without direction. The country remained in this amorphous state until Reza Khan's 1921 coup and his installation as the first Pahlevi shah in 1925.

Some Iranians believed the new ruler revived the nationalist theme that had been eclipsed in 1911, though without the accompanying liberalism of the earlier movement.[7] The constitution was restored, the middle class and the concept of *millat-i Iran* were revitalized, and a Westernizing modernization process was inaugurated. Furthermore, the Anglo-Russian power bases had been eradicated by the Bolshevik revolution and the refusal of the *majlis* to ratify the Anglo-Iranian Agreement of 1919. Reza used this altered state of Iran's relations with the great powers to develop a pragmatic foreign policy designed to preserve the country's independence. All signs pointed to profound and irreversible change.

Reza's policies certainly promoted secularization and modernization. But the degree to which they can be considered genuinely nationalist is a moot point. Reza thought of himself, and was seen by others, as a nationalist leader. Yet he preserved a number of archaic institutions, such as the centralized monarchy and a special role for Shiite Islam. Indeed, there were certain contradictions in his plans for the reconstruction of Iran. He had no ideological framework with which to develop a nationalist platform, such as that forwarded by Mustafa Kemal in Turkey. Nevertheless, the political course he pursued reflected a state-sponsored Persian nationalism, without an accompanying doctrine. His successor carried this course a step further, idealizing the pre-Islamic grandeur of Persia and exalting in a 1971 celebration the continuity of Persian monarchy dating back two and a half millennia.

This kind of regime-oriented nationalism is at variance with the liberal nationalism implicit in the position taken by Musaddiq's National front during the 1951–1953 crisis. Though the front was composed of groups with differing political beliefs, the platform endorsed by all was that the political system should be liberalized and the oil industry nationalized to eliminate foreign control. Although these themes stemmed from the 1906 revolution, in both cases no doctrine, either of liberalization or nationalism, was clearly defined or fully developed. Opinions differed as to how the political system should be made more equitable, and when nationalist sentiment went beyond mere opposition to foreign exploitation of the country's resources, it was either Persian nationalism posing as a *millat-i Iran* movement or the separatism of the non-Persian components of Iranian society.

With the restoration of the shah's authority in summer 1953, the National front and the loosely defined nationalist platform it had sponsored became politically impotent. The only remnants of the movement were a residue of middle-class support for liberalization and the attempts of some intellectuals to perpetuate the *millat-i Iran* concept, often in esoteric and somewhat metaphysical terms.[8] Overshadowing the entire sociopolitical spectrum was the image of the shah, who gradually consolidated his power over state and country under the auspices of a contrived state-sponsored nationalism designed to eliminate opposition and enhance the ruler's control of all political affairs. This nationalism was institutionalized in 1975 with the creation of the Rastakhiz (Resurgence) party as the sole legitimate political association in the country.

The final resting point of the nationalist movement in Iran, then, was an authoritarian system without a developed political philosophy or nationalist ideology beyond the very limited and often oppressive principle of monarchial supremacy combined with the shah's obsession to make Iran the dominant regional power in the Middle East. The segments of the population that approved of the regime's modernization program were keenly aware of the void in the theoretical concept of the Pahlevi state that prevented any genuine democratization. Yet this liberal contingent was itself unable to construct and propagate alternative doctrines, the growth of political ideology having been severely stunted in Iran. At best, it set forth a few partially developed ideas about *millat-i Iran*. Beyond this group lay the amorphous Iranian masses, who became increasingly anti-Western in their opposition to the regime or identified with the particularism of the non-Persian ethnic movements. In effect, nationalism in Iran was never able to mature as a concept or to achieve power as a movement. Carried by currents and circumstances beyond its control, it eventually ended as one element in the anarchy that unfolded in the late 1970s and was subsequently submerged by the tide of Islamic resurgence that swept the country under the aegis of Ayatollah Khomeini.

The Arab World

Nationalism in the Arab world developed characteristics similar to those of the parallel movements in Turkey and Iran but with distinct features related to differing circumstances. Its origins lie in the climate of reformist thought that became increasingly pervasive in the Ottoman Empire as the nineteenth century unfolded and in the resistance to the progressive colonization of many of the Arab countries during the same period.

The concept of reform in the Arab areas was first developed in an Islamic context by the *salafiyya* thinkers. Though not in any sense nationalistic initially, aside from Muhammad Abduh's special interest in Egypt and the Arabs, the *salafiyya* movement acquired an Arab orientation with a distinct anti-Turkish flavor. Abdul Rahman al-Kawakibi (1849–1903) was one of the first to blame the Ottomans for the degenerate state of Islam in the Middle East—for him the product of despotism in particular—and to suggest that the revival should be undertaken by Arabs.[9] At a later date, even pan-Islamic reformers like Muhammad Rashid Rida (1865–1935) subscribed to the idea that the reconstruction of Islam would be most effective if placed in Arab hands.[10] This preference of Arab Muslim advocates of change represents an implicit nationalist dimension in their conceptual framework. It also provided the bridge between the movement for Islamic reform and the rise of what later emerged as the transnational doctrine of pan-Arabism. The early stages of nationalism among the Arabs, however, were regional in orientation.

As Arab lands fell under European control in the late decades of the nineteenth century and the early part of the twentieth, nationalist doctrines became more politically activist and less related to Islamic issues and theoretical considerations. They were formulated in secular terms and addressed to the question of liberation from foreign control. All were regional in scope and aimed at generating a patriotic anticolonialist movement among the people of a particular country or geographic area. They had varying degrees of ideological content, but their conceptual vision of the political order to be established was limited.

Nationalism in Egypt grew out of the secularism of some of the second generation *salafiyya* intellectuals. It was also a product of the general resistance to British occupation. A number of Muhammad Abduh's disciples—especially Muhammad Farid Wajdi (1875–1954), Qasim Amin (1865–1908), and Ahmad Lutfi al-Sayyid (1872–1964)—gradually altered the concept of Islamic reform, tying it more closely to the Western understanding of modernization. As Albert Hourani put it succinctly in reference to Wajdi's work, whereas Abduh maintained "that *true* civilization is in conformity with Islam . . . in Wajdi's book we can see a subtle change of tone and emphasis, an implication that *true* Islam is in conformity with civilization."[11] Qasim Amin and Ahmad Lutfi al-Sayyid were educated in modernized Egyptian and European schools and colleges and were deeply influenced by contemporary Western thought. Despite their enormous respect for Abduh and his ideas, Islam does not play nearly as important a role in their thinking. Their model is always the high civilization that they found in the Europe of their day.

The secularism of this school of Abduh's disciples helped to create the intellectual climate and to provide some of the ideas that eventually resulted in a rudimentary doctrine of modern Egyptian nationalism. The nationalist opposition to foreign intervention had begun with the popular uprising led by Colonel Ahmad Urabi Pasha against domestic misrule and the Anglo-French dual control of the economy. This paradoxically ended in the British occupation of 1882, which produced a more concrete nationalist doctrine.

Mustafa Kamil (1874–1908) became the recognized founder of Egyptian nationalism but more as an agitator than as an ideologue.[12] Although he inspired a new patriotism, his contribution to the concept of nationalism did not go much beyond the rhetoric of romanticized love of country. For him, Egypt as fatherland became an object of devotion, the proper focus of allegiance, and the ultimate meaning of existence for its people. This expression of nationalism as sentimental attachment was later elaborated on a more sophisticated level by Ahmad Lutfi al-Sayyid.[13] Yet the idea of nationalism in Egypt never achieved the maturity found in Western political thought. Saad Zaghlul and the Wafd party he founded in 1919 tried to transform Lutfi al-Sayyid's secular liberal interpretation of Egyptian nationalism into a working political doctrine, but they were ultimately consumed by the very struggle against British rule to which they had devoted their lives. The quest for a viable political doctrine was frustrated in the process. Tawfiq al-Hakim and the pharaonists developed the idea of an Egyptian identity predating Islam by millennia as the basis of a modern political ideology, but this exceeded even the romantic nationalism of Mustafa Kamil and never addressed such issues as sovereignty, justice, and equity.[14]

Eventually, the Wafd became an oligarchic political elite, incapable of dealing effectively with the escalating social and political problems confronting Egypt. By midcentury, following over sixty years of experimentation with the idea and practice of nationalism, Egypt was as far away from a satisfactory political order as ever. What ensued were several revisionist attempts to launch the country on a constructive path.

Parallel Islamic reform and regional nationalist movements appeared in the Maghreb in the late nineteenth and early twentieth centuries.[15] The *salafiyya* idea took root in this area, and political parties were formed, including the Istiqlal party in Morocco, the Destour and Neo-Destour parties in Tunisia, and the National Liberation front in Algeria. As in Egypt, Islamic reform gave way to nationalism, in part because of the immediate problem of colonial rule. In some cases, there was a mixture of the two. The Istiqlal's founder, Allal al-Fasi, for example, was at the same time an advocate of Abduh's approach to Islamic reform and a champion of Maghreb unity and independence. Ultimately, however, the doctrines of regional or subregional nationalism prevailed over the Islamic revival movement.

Nationalism in the Maghreb never developed an adequate ideological structure beyond the anti-French liberationist motif. It also lacked a clearly defined constitutional foundation defining rights, prerogatives, and limits of power. As a result, though none of the regimes that followed the termination of French rule could be considered repressive, entrenched elites controlled the political process and ran the state. The monarchy in Morocco, Bourguiba and the Neo-Destour in Tunisia, and the National Liberation front in Algeria dominated the entire nation-building process and contained all attempts at political opposition. Despite altruistic intention in each case, monopolization of power in the formative phase blocked the active participation of the citizenry in the political system and prevented consideration of safeguards against malpractice.

Nationalism in the Fertile Crescent began as a separatist movement from Ottoman control in the eight Turkish-ruled provinces of the region. The traditional loyalty to the empire had begun to diminish in the last quarter of the nineteenth century and became more marked after the Young Turk revolution in 1908. Though some of those involved in politics sought a decentralization of the Ottoman system, several underground organizations advocated and actively sought independence.[16] Al-Qahtaniyya (named after al-Qahtan, a legendary ancestor of the Arabs) founded in 1909, al-Jamiyya al-Arabiyya al-Fatat (Young Arab society) established in 1911, and al-Ahd (covenant) created in 1914 were the most important of these organizations. Their aspirations and platforms represent an early expression of Syrian nationalism, if the concept is understood in the broadest sense as a Fertile Crescent liberation movement.

Following a prolonged correspondence with the British high commissioner in Egypt, Sir Henry McMahon, Sharif Hussein of Mecca proclaimed himself the titular leader of the Great Arab Revolt in June 1916. The platform of this insurrection among the eastern Arabs was based on al-Fatat's Damascus Protocol, and the leader of the Sharifian forces, Hussein's son Faisal, was himself a member of the Syrian underground organization.[17] The ensuing military campaign won popular support throughout the remaining Ottoman-controlled Arab provinces, and many came over to the nationalist cause. The movement nevertheless had a weakly defined program of political principles upon which the country's government was to be based, leaving a tenuous foundation for the future polity. But its success against the Turks was partly responsible for the liberation of the Arab east, where a new political tradition was inaugurated.

Despite the extension of British and French rule into the Fertile Crescent after World War I, a nation-building process did unfold. The leadership of the nationalist order became deeply involved in the continuing struggle for independence from the colonial powers, but it also tried to shape the political orientation of the component subregions, now artificially divided by administrative boundaries imposed by the League of Nations.

Mostly of middle-class and upper-middle-class origins, the members of this first generation of the nationalist elite had either been educated in Europe or America or gone to one of the Western schools and colleges in the area. Their orientation was secular, and they sought to emulate the Western tradition of liberalism and felt committed to the principles of parliamentary democracy. Though the Muslims among them did not relinquish their religious identity, many held Islam responsible for the problems confronting Middle Eastern society. For this reason, they often consciously or unconsciously replaced Islam with nationalism as their principal article of faith. They considered themselves dedicated patriots and champions of the struggle for liberation, as well as founding fathers of the countries they were trying to free from colonial rule. It was a self-image of reasonableness, enlightenment, respectability, and devotion to public service on behalf of the national interests they represented.

Though the first generation nationalists in the Fertile Crescent—especially the National bloc in Syria—were ardent in their endeavors to achieve the genuine independence of the mandated territories, they were gradually drawn into a narrow, particularist frame of reference that transformed them into representatives of various vested interests and the political-territorial status quo. As their commitment to the general welfare of their constituencies faded, they became increasingly inclined to reach compromise agreements with the colonial powers, helping to preserve a high degree of British and French influence in the area. This led in the 1930s to their being discredited as responsible wardens of the nationalist order.

An important shortcoming of the early nationalist elite throughout much of the Arab world was its general inability to communicate effectively with the commonalty. Virtually all the institutions it sought to establish and the political symbols it used to convey ideas were derived from Western liberalism and had little Islamic content. Composed of people who had visited the West, been educated in Western institutions, and could speak and read one or more European languages, the elite had lost touch with many aspects of its own native culture and not infrequently held it in contempt. This created a barrier between the ruling elite and the masses, a schism in the body social that was destined to unseat the early parties initially and later to engender a much broader alienation from the nationalist order in general.

The problems surrounding the initial phase of nationalism in the Arab world led to the emergence of revisionist schools of thought that sought to redefine the nationalist doctrine in more idealistic terms. The most significant development was the rise of pan-Arabism as a political creed. Movement toward inter-Arab cooperation had been initiated in the 1930s by the convention of congresses designed to address the problem of Zionism. This created a certain receptivity to the idea of a common Arab nationality which, though implicit in the thought of some Syrian nationalists, had never been systematically formulated. The most important person to articulate pan-Arab ideology was Sati al-Husri (1880–1968).

Al-Husri's Arabism was the product of the demise of the Ottoman Empire, to which he had originally given his complete allegiance. It was also stimulated by his exposure to the literature of European nationalism. Though the son of Syrian parents, he grew up in a Turkish environment and was consequently a native speaker of Turkish. His father was an Ottoman civil servant, and he himself became an educational administrator in Istanbul. A loyal Ottoman until the end of World War I, he had played no role in the separatist movement in the Fertile Crescent provinces. With the collapse of the empire, however, he redirected his former patriotism and became an ardent Arab nationalist. The transition was so dramatic that he was accused by some of exaggerating his new political faith to minimize his lack of participation in the Arab cause during the war.[18]

Whether contrived or not, al-Husri's doctrine of Arab nationalism became the theoretical basis of the pan-Arab ideology popularized by the Baath party, the Nasserites, and others in the 1940s and 1950s. Al-Husri's own conceptualism, though it was widely acclaimed and had a profound impact on Arab political thought, was founded on broad generalizations and contained some serious oversights.

The central premise is that nationality, which stems mainly from a common language and historical experience, is the most important form of human association. Individuals discover meaning and purpose in life by identifying with the interests and destiny of the nation to which they belong. Therefore, true freedom does not come from constitutional guarantees or parliamentary democracy but from discovery of the national ethos and the achievement of national unity.[19] Al-Husri derived this notion mainly from the German nationalist thinkers, especially Johann Fichte, though he placed less emphasis on race than on culture. His own personal Arab identity, however, was more ethnic than linguistic, as he always spoke Arabic with a strong Turkish accent.

The romanticism inherent in German nationalist thought is evident in al-Husri's ideas. In this respect, he inherited a problem from them that was aptly summarized by William Cleveland:

> What Otto Pflanza has called "the diversionary influence of nationalism" whereby nationalist sentiments tend to channel appeals away from certain fundamental issues of social justice and political freedom was typical of Arab nationalism at this time and . . . was particularly evident in al-Husri's works.[20]

Any doctrine that glorifies a collective entity and suggests that the individuals within it can find fulfillment only through submission and dedication to the whole is a powerful theme in German and other forms of romantic nationalism. Its cardinal weakness is its insensitivity to the needs, identity, and aspirations of the individual, an attribute that inclines it in the direction of ideological rigidity and autocratic politics. Cleveland quoted al-Husri on this subject: "Patriotism and nationalism above and before all else, even above and before freedom." Cleveland was then forced to conclude that "aspects of totalitarianism certainly seem to be implicit in al-Husri's concept of Arab nationalism and unity."[21] Though he did not detect any preference for dictatorship or tendency to glorify the state, he found a primary weakness in al-Husri's doctrine of pan-Arab nationalism—its failure to specify the character of the sociopolitical order it was designed to bring into existence.

Another defect in the conceptual framework of the pan-Arab idea was its reliance on idealist and sometimes fallible interpretations of history. Cleveland saw a clear indication of this defect in al-Husri's thought: "He presented only that which was propitious to his cause. He had an objective to which he rigidly adhered, and if he sometimes distorted or simplified history, it was because his objective was best served by such a presentation."[22]

The combination of romantic nationalism, an impoverished political philosophy, and a manipulative approach to history rendered pan-Arab ideology extremely vulnerable to the test of time. What Sati al-Husri bequeathed to those who tried to put the doctrine into practice was too removed from the realities of Arab politics and the requirements of equitable order to provide the basis for any durable polity. Those who tried to elaborate the theory failed to address its inherent flaws, and those who made it the basis of state policy often used it to conceal their own attempts to monopolize power. In the final analysis, it remained an emotive theoretical framework without an accompanying set of stabilizing political principles.

Other pan-Arab ideologues, such as Abdul Rahman al-Bazzaz (1913–1973) and Michel Aflaq (1910–), expanded al-Husri's concepts but very much in the same vein and without adding the needed remedies. Al-Bazzaz developed the questionable idea that Islam and Arab nationalism were inseparably linked by history, insisting that Muhammad had stimulated the revival of the Arab nation.[23] Aflaq, though himself a Christian, saw a similar connection between Islam and Arabism. He regarded Islam as an Arab movement and held that "The message of Islam is to create an Arab humanism."[24]

Aflaq founded the Baath party in 1943, incorporating the pan-Arab position as its fundamental platform and associating it with the concept of Arab socialism when the merger with Akram Hourani's Socialist party was effected in 1950. The institutionalization of ideas originally systematized by Sati al-Husri did not, however, promote a more flexible and politically responsible pan-Arabism but an increasingly doctrinaire ideology that became a vehicle of state control when the Baath came to power in Syria and Iraq in the 1960s.

Pan-Arabism was also established as an official doctrine in Egypt when Gamal Abdul Nasser emerged as the country's leader following the July 1952 revolution. Convinced that the Arab countries were linked to each other by historical ties, contemporary interdependence, and common dangers, Abdul Nasser assumed the role of a charismatic champion of Arab unity, relinquishing the previous tradition of Egyptian nationalism. He also embraced Arab socialism as the only policy capable of achieving social equity. In these respects, he challenged the status quo and launched a revisionist nationalism that caught the imagination of millions, most of whom looked to a transformation of Egypt and of the Arab world.

Abdul Nasser's socialist pan-Arabism was based more on good intentions related to a desire for dramatic and far-reaching change than on a thoughtfully visualized and viable program of sociopolitical transition. Though committed to certain ideals concerning the identity and destiny of the Arabs, its political objectives were often not very practical. As a platform, its main function was to serve as a vehicle of rhetorical communication between the ruling elite and the masses in Egypt. Ultimately, Nasserism came to be regarded by intellectuals in particular as an unsuccessful attempt to solve the problems besetting the Arabs through a combination of a subtle reinterpretation of Islamic reformism, Arab nationalism, and socialism.[25] In inter-Arab politics, it began to lose its popularity after the 1967 Arab-Israeli war. By the late 1970s, Fouad Ajami summarized the now widely held view of many of his contemporaries in his "The End of Pan-Arabism."[26] The emphasis throughout most of the Arab world had shifted to pragmatism, regionalism, and useful bilateral or group alliances.

The revisionist generation, which sought to correct the perceived failures of nationalism as originally instated in the Arab countries, was itself as inept and short sighted as the one that preceded it. It was caught in the same kind of dilemma that had rendered the earlier generation incapable of dealing constructively and satisfactorily with the real world but for different reasons. Though dedicated to a viable nationalist reconstruction, its members had difficulty in resolving the problems that had impeded the nation-building process, despite some achievements in creating greater social integration. Alternate doctrines, such as that of the regionally oriented Syrian nationalist movement, were equally ineffective because their appeal was limited and they were never able to make headway in the political environment.

The period beginning in the 1970s witnessed an increasing disenchantment with ideology in general and a corresponding preference for practical approaches to the fulfillment of more limited aspirations. Yet the pragmatist leaders, such as Anwar Sadat and Hafiz al-Asad, were themselves disappointing because their policies were perceived as serving the interests of only certain segments of their respective societies. This limited perspective led many to look for new answers in the doctrines of the emerging Islamic resurgence movement.

4

The Islamic
Reconstructionist Response

Turning to Islam for solutions to a perceived state of public disorder was a natural response among Muslims because of Islamdom's traditional political orientation. Indeed, Islamic revivalism had played a major role in the entire reform movement in the Middle East, dating back to the nineteenth century. The dominant theme among religious reconstructionists in the early phase was the Islamic modernist idea of evaluating existing institutions and seeking an appropriate and effective revision of them from an intellectual Islamic perspective. This school, however, never had a significant impact on political developments or broad popular backing. Its implicit commitment to Islamic humanism and its familiarity with the modern world and the challenges it posed consequently did not become the basis of the Islamic renewal (*tajdid*) movement. When the nationalist trend began to diminish, the neofundamentalist interpretation became dominant.

Though also oriented toward Islamic reform, the neofundamentalists were more literalist and political and less inclined to humanism and openmindedness than their modernist counterparts. They nevertheless exercised much greater influence on their contemporaries when circumstances thrust them into the mainstream of Middle East politics. This influence resulted partly because their own opposition to the established nationalist order coincided with a growing popular disenchantment with the status quo, allowing them to become spokespeople for the antiregime movement in several countries. They also had an advantage in the relative simplicity of their platform, which was based on a frontal attack on secular nationalism and a literalist Islamic political program as the remedy for the problems confronting Middle Eastern society.

The residue of unanswered questions left by the neofundamentalist interpretation of Islam as the solution to perceived sociopolitical disorder related primarily to the exercise of power and emergence of a global culture. Assuming that the reinstitution of the *sharia* and an Islamic system of government would create ideal conditions, the neofundamentalists failed to consider abuse of authority as a possibility and established no safeguards against it. They also did not take into account the degree to which Westernization had altered the character and orientation of society in the Middle East and the rest of the Third World, giving rise to an international cosmopolitanism. This oversight prevented them from looking at the alternative of reviving Islam in the context of cultural synthesis, which may be the only option realistically open to those in search of Islamic renewal. Paradoxically, this implicitly opened the door to a reconsideration of the now eclipsed but nevertheless extremely relevant Islamic modernist approach to change.

Islamic Modernism

The *salafiyya* movement introduced by Jamal al-Din al-Afghani and Muhammad Abduh was the most prominent of the Islamic modernist schools of thought in the Middle East. It was devoted to an unrestricted reexamination of Islamic tradition in quest of solutions to contemporary problems. It emphasized the revival of intellectual analysis and the spirit of free inquiry in the task of Islamic reconstruction. Parallel interpretations appeared among some of the Young Ottoman thinkers, Namik Kemal in particular.

Jamal al-Din al-Afghani (1839–1897) was perhaps the first Middle Eastern intellectual to deal in a comprehensive way with the multiple problem of the West as a political and cultural challenge. A pan-Islamic revivalist, he was primarily concerned with rescuing Islamdom as a civilization by recovering its cultural heritage and the solidarity of the *umma* that had existed in the inaugural period.[1] The Muslim world was under attack and could defend itself only by reactivating the scientific and philosophical traditions of the Islamic legacy. This process would revive the inner strength of Islam and enable Muslim societies to rebuild themselves and bring an end to the European intrusion.

Muhammad Abduh (1849–1905), who refined and elaborated the *salafiyya* idea, was the principal architect of early Islamic modernism as a systematic doctrine. His perspective, however, was less pan-Islamic than that of al-Afghani, since he had a particular interest in Egypt and the Arabs. In this respect, his thought remains at the focus of the current confrontation between secular nationalism and Islamic revivalism in the Middle East. Figuratively speaking, he stood at the meeting place of the two dominant crosscurrents in nineteenth-century Egypt: "the traditional Islamic spirit, resisting all change" and "the spirit of the younger generation, accepting all change and all the ideas of modern Europe."[2]

Acknowledging the fact and irreversibility of change brought about by the introduction of Western culture in the Middle East, he sought to preserve Islamic principles in the modern context by reviving the intellectual resiliency that had characterized the early centuries of Islam.

Abduh devoted particular attention to redefining Islam for his contemporaries. Like many Middle Eastern intellectuals, he thought the Islam of his own time represented a degenerate form of the original. The main problems were the prevalence of despotism and *taqlid*, the slavish adherence to established doctrines that virtually precluded any significant independent thought. The combination of a corrupt sociopolitical order and a petrified religious tradition had rendered the Muslims of the Middle East and elsewhere incapable of coping with the imposing challenges of the modern world. The solution, therefore, lay not in revolution or random attempts at the reform of existing institutions but in an intellectual awakening based on the restoration of *ijtihad*. This approach in itself would open the door to a rediscovery of the real tenets of Islam, of the values and concepts that had been responsible for the great accomplishments of the past. As the key to renewal, it would also eventually lead to a sound social and political reconstruction.

The most important imperatives for modern Muslims were, in Abduh's view, to liberate themselves from intellectual constraints and recover the understanding of Islam that had existed among the *salaf*, or members of the original *umma*. These would make it possible to revive the traditions and outlook of the high Islamic civilization of the golden age, a heritage completely capable of addressing the problems of the current period. As Abduh succinctly put it, "I raised my voice to summon to two important matters . . . to free the mind from the chains of belief on authority, and to understand the religion (of Islam) as the early generation understood it, before the appearance of divisions among them, and to return to the original sources of the branches of the sciences (of Islam) in order to attain a proper knowledge of them."[3]

Muhammad Abduh's concerns were not, however, restricted to the reconstruction of present-day Islam through the use of the past as a model. He was also deeply interested in the debate over science and religion in nineteenth-century Europe and its relevance for contemporary Muslims.[4] He had read some of the English and French books on the subject and was certainly influenced by Western thinkers, though he tried to refute their arguments. His ultimate position on the whole question of science and religion was that Islam had resolved the problem in earlier centuries by combining an affirmation of the human intellect and the scientific spirit with a faith in the transcendence and moral supremacy of God.

What is more important, however, is the Westernized dimension of Abduh's thought and personality. The profundity and appropriateness of his message were of lasting importance and will almost certainly come under reconsideration in the foreseeable future. The problem lay in the fact that he and the other *salafiyya* thinkers constituted an intellectual elite, committed to the revival of the best in the Islamic tradition but simultaneously oriented in terms of Western conceptualism. There were always questions regarding the degree to which it is possible to reconstruct and imitate an imagined model of early Islam to provide the guidelines for contemporary change. Another issue was the extent to which Abduh and his associates were trying to reconcile Islam with modern Western thought, selecting those aspects of the Islamic tradition most compatible with European interpretive systems rather than employing purely Islamic criteria. These unresolved matters do not diminish the value of the *salafiyya* idea, but they do have to be taken into consideration at some point.

In dealing with the various ramifications of Islamic reconstruction, it is clearly absurd to suggest that the only valid Islam is what came down to the present in a degenerate or stagnant form. A rich and comprehensive religious culture such as Islam must be seen as a growing legacy that accrues various attributes in time. Similarly, it is perfectly natural and desirable for those who transmit the culture from one generation to the next to correct aberrations, reform degenerate practices, and revitalize the dominant humanistic themes. In any event, there is no question that Islam in the Middle East had by the nineteenth century reached the point where it could no longer afford to leave itself vulnerable to external intrusion.

With regard to the question of cultural borrowing, the introduction of Western traditions in an Islamic milieu is neither unprecedented nor representative of the intrusion of elements alien to Islam. The Islamic synthesis of the medieval period was characterized by the incorporation of many foreign cultures, including European, within an Islamic framework. Moreover, the civilizations of Islam and the West have common origins. As Marshall Hodgson pointed out,

> the roots of Islamicate civilization are largely the same as those of Occidental civilization: the urban commercial tradition of the Fertile Crescent, the Hebrew religious challenge, the classical Greek philosophical and scientific culture. Hence for Westerners (and for all who at least partly share now in the Occidental heritage), the Islamicate forms a sister civilization, like yet very different. . . . [5]

In launching the *salafiyya* movement, Jamal al-Din al-Afghani and Muhammad Abduh inaugurated the quest for actual reform among Muslims of the Middle East. Though the changes they had in mind did not materialize, the interest in change they generated did revolutionize the sociopolitical outlook of concerned educated people and eventually led to extensive revision of the status quo. Although they were unable to reach average people below the level of the intellectual elite, they laid the groundwork for the Islamic resurgence movements that began to emerge in the mid-twentieth century. The style and tone of the modernists were, however, far more circumspect and sophisticated than those of the militants of later generations.

Muhammad Abduh had always feared that the modernization process would create a rift in Middle Eastern societies between a segment of the population that was increasingly drawn to Western customs and thought patterns and the traditional masses that continued to act and look at the world from an Islamic perspective.[6] This apprehension turned out to be well founded, and ultimately a conflict developed between the Westernized secular nationalists and the militant Islamic groups and organizations. What Abduh did not foresee was that a movement of Islamic repoliticization, quite removed from his own approach to Islamic reform and enlisting the support of the alienated commonalty, would have a bitter confrontation with the advocates of reconstruction along Western lines.

Namik Kemal (1840–1888), the celebrated Turkish Young Ottoman publicist, developed doctrines that combined Islamic and Western traditions in much the same way as the *salafiyya* thinkers, though with greater emphasis on political change.[7] He more than any other sought to create a synthesis of Islamic law and Western parliamentary practice based on the concepts of natural law and popular sovereignty. His main argument was that people come to understand proper political order and juridical procedure through divine revelation and through accurate perception of the good (*husn*) that God has infused into nature. From this premise, he developed a theory of popular sovereignty and constitutionality that was presumably in complete harmony with the *sharia* and the concept of the Islamic state.

Namik Kemal was really addressing the question of whether it is possible to be Islamic and "modern" at the same time, and he arrived at an affirmative answer. The issue of the compatibility of the Islamic and Western secular views of the world, the state, justice, and interpersonal relations was as applicable in the case of the Young Ottomans as it was with the *salafiyya* thinkers. Namik Kemal did not see any fundamental conflict between the two systems. Yet he himself was strongly influenced by European political doctrines and institutions, inclining him to reinterpret Islam from a Western perspective. Once again, the question is what constitutes genuine fidelity to Islam. There is a fine line between constructive elaboration and innovation (*bida*), the former always accepted by Muslims and the latter rejected as heretical.

Namik Kemal, Muhammad Abduh, and the whole school of nineteenth-century Islamic modernism were deeply committed to devising a system of change consistent with what they saw as the best in the Islamic tradition. They felt free to borrow whatever they wanted from the West, insisting that in doing so they were always employing an Islamic frame of reference. Without meaning to, however, they were in fact promoting a comprehensive secularization of their societies that had little relationship to traditional Islam. The reaction against precisely this secularization in the following century produced a very different kind of Islamic revivalism, one that was neofundamentalist and militant in its orientation. Though the new Islamic resurgence movement took some of its ideas from the *salafiyya* concept of using early Islam as the model for reform in the present, it broke with the intellectual elitist approach of Muhammad Abduh and the other modernists. Preaching an Islamic populism, it took its doctrines to the street and actively sought a revolutionary following among the masses.

The Transition to Militancy

The militant Islamic resurgence organizations that became increasingly significant as the nationalist order declined in popularity in the middle decades of the twentieth century assumed a political role the Islamic modernists had never been able to achieve. Their ideology ultimately came to be used as a major vehicle of dissent against the status quo. It represents an alternative to the radical leftist mode of opposition, but it is capable of enlisting far greater support from the various alienated segments of the population. Usually referred to as either Islamic re-politicization, militancy, neofundamentalism, or resurgency, the movement is still relatively amorphous, undefined, and disorganized. It also remains somewhat of an enigma. Yet its influence is constantly spreading throughout the Middle East, touching the lives of millions.

The idea of Islamic resistance to the status quo is appealing to dissident elements in the Middle East for several reasons. The secular nationalist experiment, which had left many disenchanted, started with the de-politicization of Islam, dramatically inaugurated by the abolition of the sultanate-caliphate in Turkey between 1922 and 1924. Also in the 1920s a book on Islam and political authority authored by the Egyptian writer, Ali Abdul Raziq, created a rather tempestuous exchange of views.[8] Abdul Raziq maintained that Muhammad's mission was prophetic rather than political and that the *umma* was basically a spiritual community. He also argued that since for the most part the caliphates of the past had led to corruption and malpractice, the institution should now be discontinued. Though a conference was convened at al-Azhar University in Cairo to debate the issue, no action to revive the institution was recommended. Despite the expression of considerable support for preserving the caliphate at the time, the opposition to it became increasingly widespread and interest in the subject has waned in the Arab world and elsewhere ever since.

Yet the great periods of Islamic history were those when power resided in the caliph, who ruled over a political empire. This fact led the Islamic resurgence organizations to view the reconstruction of political Islam as the solution to contemporary problems. It was not only a way of challenging the status quo but the only means of purifying the corrupt Islamic societies of the present and reinstating the values upon which the religion is based.

Equally important was the relevance of Islamic symbolism in the context of the anti-Western trend that developed as part of the overall revolt against the secular-nationalist order. Islam had begun as a purifying religion, based on Muhammad's rejection of false gods and distorted values. Awareness of this aspect was heightened at a time when many had come to regard the Middle East as polluted by Western secular culture. The West was identified as antireligious and antisocial, contemptuous of the moral principles essential to the preservation of a virtuous community. The cult of the individual, manifested in the decadence of its atomistic youth culture,[9] was in direct defiance of the traditional Islamic view of society, which had always been based on interlocking family relationships and the idea of the ordered *umma*. The spiritual crisis evident in Europe and the United States was the product of the half-truths inherent in Western secularism, humanism, rationalism, and nationalism.[10] Circumstances had therefore thrust Islam into a corrective role. This was the only protection against contaminating influences for Muslims of the Middle East.

Those who turned to Islam to express dissent took particular issue with the doctrine of nationalism, considered the fundamental Western institution and the most dangerous of the non-Islamic traditions infecting the Middle East in modern times. Nationalism was a form of collective self-worship, totally devoid of religious content, in which the material interests of the nation-state community were paramount. In this sense, it represented the ultimate form of idolatry and was particularly diabolical because of the technological and military power the West had acquired. Thus, modern Islam was axiomatically at war not only with the West but with nationalism as well.

Another appealing aspect of Islamic resurgence was the fact that for well over a millennium Islam has been the focus of Middle Eastern identity and the sociopolitical orientation passed down through the generations. The gradual eclipse of this identity by the Westernization process had created a psychocultural void that troubled many. Hence, the rediscovery of an Islamic ethos was often received as a kind of panacea for the various dislocations that had beset the Middle East. One of the major problems was the split between the Westernized culture of the elite and the popular culture of the masses,[11] and the rejuvenation of Islam seemed an appropriate way of mending this schism in the body social. The Islamic emphasis on the equality of the believers and the capacity of Islam to be many things to many people were the inherent catalytic agents.

There is enormous variety in the degree to which Middle Easterners influenced by the revival of political Islam are aware of the specific issues at stake or the social dynamics behind the appeal of the resurgence movement. Certainly a large number of the rank and file see the whole situation in relatively simplistic terms. They are aware of their grievances against the established power elite, their anger and frustration, their alienation from the Westernized intelligentsia. Islam, by contrast, is genuine and reassuring; it can triumph against abuse and provide the foundations of justice and equity. It can purify the cultural contamination introduced by the West through its own guidelines to wholesome social interaction. It can also generate political strength by encouraging unity.

Others support the movement less because of attraction to Islamic symbols than realization that Islam is the only viable vehicle of dissent. Those segments of the secularized middle classes that oppose the established regimes on political grounds often find that the only avenue of active opposition open to them is to support militant Islamic organizations. Aware of the potential power inherent in movements that galvanize the masses, they try to work with and through them to check or overthrow the ruling elites. But in this case, their involvement in Islamic resistance is based on pragmatism rather than commitment to religious values and principles.

The leadership of the neofundamentalist movement is composed of members of the clerical class, an even larger number of activist Muslim laymen, and political figures who combine revolutionary doctrines with Islamic symbols. The prominent among the *ulama* are not all politically oriented. Probably a majority are conservative and inclined by tradition to maintain a distance from or to cooperate with those in authority. But those inspired to challenge the secularism and corruption of the established regimes often find their way into leadership positions in the resurgence movement. In this role, they become dedicated champions of the new *jihad*, the war against Western culture and political influence. Uplifted by their deliverance from obscurity, they respond to the demand for an Islamic revolt by developing elaborate doctrines on the neofundamentalist position and by fashioning a unique charismatic pose. They enunciate the message of Islam in the idiom of the common person.

The lay Islamic revolutionaries work with the clerical leaders to create a composite of Islamic sociotheological precepts and modern revolutionary ideology. Using the language of secular dissent and the political symbols of Islam, they articulate in understandable and coherent terms a platform of activist opposition geared to the sense of outrage that has developed among the masses. They provide a link between the people and the politicized *ulama* and serve as a revolutionary vanguard of the resurgence movement.

The underlying force that has made Islamic neofundamentalism a significant dimension of the Middle East political scene is the impelling need of the societies in the area to fill in some meaningful way the vacuum created by the failure of nationalism to meet the challenges of modernization. Islam offered many symbolic solutions to the problem, especially those dealing with purification. Though most fundamentalist and neofundamentalist interpretations of renewal (*tajdid*) do not include the messianic concept of the Mahdi, the militant organizations of the 1970s and 1980s acquired a millenarian aura with Mahdist overtones.[12] This interpretation arose because, in John Voll's words, "in times of perceived crisis or the failure of other Islamic modes, the apocalyptic style of revival is a popular one."[13] The resurgence movement therefore gathered a broad following among those no longer willing to accept the inability of the nationalist elites to prevent external encroachment, harness corruption, and establish the guidelines of sociopolitical stability. This phenomenon represents the urgent quest of large segments of the population to seek out and follow those who in some way or another can serve as symbols and agents of a corrective revolution, a return to basics in a time of chaos.

The appeal of neofundamentalism notwithstanding, the approach of the Islamic militants to contemporary difficulties and to the whole question of reform is fraught with intrinsic problems. In reviving the political dimension of Islam as a reaction to perceived internal and external challenges without including the more important humanist elements, they raised the level of angry emotionalism and diminished the prospects of a broader and richer Islamic reconstruction. Seldom mindful of Islam's past political shortcomings or of its humanist attributes, they ran the risk of recapitulating the mistakes of earlier centuries and falling short of the changes to which they aspired. They were so intent on confronting what they considered demonic foreign forces and on purifying their own societies of Western influences that they lost the ability to analyze the implications of everything around them and of their own actions. In a sense, they ensnared themselves in a dilemma of generalizations and contradictions that cannot really be resolved without recourse to more profound Islamic perspectives.

Islamic Neofundamentalism

Islamic resurgence as we know it today began with the formation of the Society of Muslim Brothers (Jamiyyat al-Ikhwan al-Muslimin) by Hasan al-Banna (1906–1949) in 1928. Egypt was in many respects the most logical place for such a movement to take root. The British occupation in 1882 had been a particularly dramatic episode in the history of the Eastern Question, and for many Muslims it symbolized the basic aspects of the intense confrontation between Western imperialism and Islam. An irresponsible ruling elite had got the country into debt, and its way of dealing with the problem was to borrow from Britain and France. This policy had completely undermined Egypt's sovereignty and brought on a popular uprising under Colonel Ahmad Urabi Pasha. But the whole affair had ended with the British takeover and decades of foreign rule and cultural intrusion.

Another important fact about Egypt was the role it had played in Islamic affairs. It was not only the largest Arabic-speaking Muslim country but also the site of the most prestigious university of Islamic scholarship, al-Azhar. It had been the seat of illustrious dynasties as well and was renowned for its many famous Islamic monuments. All the component imagery made this particular country a microcosmic reflection of the most important things happening in a Muslim world struggling to meet the formidable challenges of modern times.

What directly precipitated the rise of neofundamentalism was the dominance of the secular-nationalist leadership in the fight for Egyptian independence. The political doctrines of Mustafa Kamil, Saad Zaghlul, and the Wafd party had little Islamic content and were strongly influenced by Western nationalist models. Though it had the support of many Egyptians, not until 1936 was the Wafd party able to reach a compromise agreement with Britain, and even that was far from satisfactory. In the meantime, the internal trend toward secularism had noticeably changed the cultural orientation of the country, compounding the problem of the British presence for those who sought to preserve Egypt's Islamic traditions.

In this context Hasan al-Banna developed the ideology and organizational foundation of the Muslim Brotherhood. As a schoolteacher in Ismailiyya, al-Banna had become acutely aware of the British military presence in Egypt, and this background had some influence on his general outlook.[14] His central concern was to analyze the reasons for the decline of Islam in Egypt and elsewhere and to arrive at a comprehensive and effective remedy. He was consciously close to the *salafiyya* thinkers but wanted to amplify their ideas and ignite an interest in reform among the people at large.

Al-Banna traced the political disintegration of Islam back to the Umayyad Caliphate, which produced the first in a series of corrupt polities extending to the present.[15] Ultimately, misrule undermined the viability of the Islamic state and led to foreign intervention and imperialism. The external domination that followed had a divisive influence on Muslim countries, encouraging factionalism, exploitation, and the introduction of alien cultures. Al-Banna saw twentieth century Egypt as a society that had been degraded by the condescension of the imperialists and was gradually slipping away from its Islamic heritage because the dominant classes had fallen under the spell of Westernism and lost all sense of responsibility for the welfare of their own people.

Though al-Banna admired the principles of Western democracy, he felt that the West itself had been corrupted by its preoccupation with individualism.[16] This had led initially to selfishness, class conflict, and the breakdown of the family and then to monopolization of power and imperialism. The revolutionary trends of modern Europe were, for al-Banna, an indication of the unrest caused by the moral decadence of Western culture.

Al-Banna's immediate concern was to find a way of extricating Egypt from its own predicament. The fundamental goal was to replace the existing state of disorder with a regenerative "Islamic order" (*al-nizam al-Islami*).[17] Like the *salafiyya* thinkers, al-Banna believed that a vital step in this direction was to analyze the whole question of how to deal with the challenges of the contemporary world from an Islamic perspective. Often referred to as the reopening of the doors of *ijtihad*, this approach essentially meant the construction of a conceptual framework with which to lay the foundations of an Islamic sociopolitical system. But although the *salafiyya* movement did not go beyond this theoretical starting point, Hasan al-Banna was a committed activist. Emphasizing the idea of *tajdid*,[18] he carried his message to the common people of Egypt and instilled in his followers a sense of dedication and purpose.

Al-Banna's personal charisma and talent for developing and transmitting ideas drew Egyptians to his ideology of Islamic revival. He idealized what he called the "perfection of Islam,"[19] based on mutual respect, peace, social justice, knowledge, and piety. Muslims did not need Western institutions and ideologies, though they could use such systems as parliamentary democracy, for example, if they organized them within an Islamic framework. The major principles of Islamic polity he advocated were that the Quran should be the basis of law, that government should function by consultation (*shura*), and that the rulers should be considered leaders bound by Islamic precepts and the popular will. He also believed that citizens should have guaranteed rights and be allowed to take part in the political process.

The main tasks confronting modern Egypt were, in al-Banna's view, to end all forms of political domination by the West, to check the spread of Western culture, and to replace the existing class structure with a genuine Islamic order. He devoted particular attention to some of the subtle distinctions between Western and Islamic conceptualism in order to provide a sound framework for the construction of an ideology designed to accomplish these tasks. On the subject of nationalism, which had captured the popular imagination in Egypt, he warned against the Western secular version because it deified the self-contained and self-interested nation-state. Nationalism as the collective struggle of a Muslim society against foreign control was acceptable, as was the simple love of one's homeland and people.[20]

Richard Mitchell pointed out that al-Banna saw a significant difference between various forms of *wataniyya* (devotion to one's country) and *qawmiyya* (devotion to one's people).[21] Wholesome *wataniyya* and *qawmiyya* included honoring one's homeland and the desire to preserve its independence, pride in one's social identity, and participation in constructive common endeavors. The corrupt varieties of these concepts included factionalism, the lust for power and aggrandizement, and the vaunting of race or type. Al-Banna also insisted that a Muslim's ultimate loyalty must be to the Islamic *umma*, and he took issue with Arab and Egyptian nationalism because they were Western, secular, and racist. He accepted the movement for Arab unity only insofar as it was related to the broader quest for Islamic liberation and revival. Hence, he was ideologically committed to a transnational Islamic renaissance that was in conflict with all varieties of particularism.

This Islamism, with all its universalist orientation, ran directly counter to the nationalism that had taken root in Egypt and other parts of the Middle East. Though the two movements shared a strong anti-imperalist leaning, they differed sharply on the question of using Western institutional models. The nationalists did not hesitate to copy the West because of the utilitarian advantages in so doing, while the Islamic neofundamentalists felt that the ultimate source of the Muslim world's contemporary problems was the infusion of European culture at the expense of Islamic tradition. In this vein, Hasan al-Banna took an interest in the idea of Easternism (*sharqiyya*), which posited an inevitable conflict between Asia and the West and heralded the quest of the Eastern peoples to restore their self-respect.[22]

An important contributor to the ideology of the Muslim Brotherhood was Sayyid Qutb (1906–1966). He joined the society just after the founder's death in 1949, but he elaborated some of al-Banna's ideas and had a strong influence on contemporary Islamic activist thought throughout the Middle East. As one who was initially attracted to Western methodology and conceptualism and then experienced a pronounced disenchantment with Europe and the United States because of their anti-Arab and pro-Israeli inclinations, Qutb adopted as the dominant theme of his thought hostility toward the West and a recourse to Islam as a vehicle of regenerating self-respect.[23] His thinking was strongly influenced by the Pakistani neofundamentalist theologian, Sayyid Abul Ala Mawdudi (1903–1979).

The eviction of the Palestinians and the establishment of Israel had deeply troubled Hasan al-Banna and remained a concern of the Muslim Brotherhood thereafter. But during a trip to the United States in 1949 Sayyid Qutb was shocked by what he perceived as a broad backing of Israel throughout the country and a generally negative opinion of the Arabs. His conclusion was that people in the West looked at the Middle East and Islam with condescension and had little regard for the rights and dignity of Third World inhabitants. The only way Muslims could recover their self-respect and protect themselves from exploitation, therefore, was to develop an Islamic ideology and build their political systems on it. Muslims were faced with a choice between copying foreign institutions and customs, which would only compound their problems, or recognizing the uniqueness of Islamic culture and reaping the rewards of reconstructing it in the modern world.[24]

Sayyid Qutb interpreted Islam as a liberating force and looked to a revolutionary Islamic revival that would transform the condition of Muslims in Egypt and elsewhere. He thought that well-meaning but vague programs of reform were totally unable to deal with the degenerate state of most Muslim societies. What was needed was profound and comprehensive change, removing all forms of alien influence and establishing a unified Islamic polity. He injected an even more pronounced militancy into the ideology of the Muslim Brotherhood than is evident in the doctrines of Hasan al-Banna. In this respect, he was an important link between the society itself and the radical splinter groups that have emerged in recent times.

The central concept in Sayyid Qutb's activist doctrine is that Muslims have always been confronted—perhaps more today than at any other time—with the threat of *jahiliyya* (ignorance) against which they have to wage *jihad*, or holy war.[25] In traditional Islamic parlance, the term *jahiliyya* was used to refer to the age of ignorance that preceded the advent of Islam. Using ideas derived from Mawdudi,[26] Qutb elaborated this concept into a comprehensive ideology for the contemporary Islamic resurgence movement. His description of the problem is very strongly stated:

> We are . . . surrounded by jahiliyya society today, which is of the same nature as it was during the first period of Islam, perhaps a little deeper. Our whole environment, people's beliefs and ideas, habits and art, rules and laws—is jahiliyya, even to the extent that what we consider to be Islamic culture, Islamic sources, Islamic philosophy and Islamic thought are also constructs of jahiliyya.[27]

The solution is equally dramatic:

> We must . . . free ourselves from the clutches of jahili society, jahili concepts, jahili traditions and jahili leadership. Our mission is not to compromise with the practices of jahili society, nor can we be loyal to it. . . . Our aim is first to change ourselves so that we may later change the society.[28]

Qutb's analysis of the inherent evils of *jahili* societies emphasizes their invariable preference for political systems based on servitude, "one man's lordship over another."[29] This theme struck a sensitive chord in Egypt and other Middle Eastern countries where alienation from the secular-nationalist order had made many in the underprivileged classes receptive to charges that the political elite was exploiting the common people. The desire to take action against the status quo was encouraged by Qutb's insistence that Islam had never been defensive but rather "a movement to wipe out tyranny and introduce true freedom to mankind. . . . The jihad of Islam is to secure complete freedom for every man throughout the world by releasing him from servitude to other human beings so that he may serve God."[30] This applied even within nominally Islamic countries such as Egypt because "all the existing so-called 'Muslim' societies are also jahili societies."[31]

Sayyid Qutb's attitude toward the West is distinctly hostile. Contrasted with Islamic science, which was always related to God's guidance, "the entire scientific movement in Europe started with Godlessness. . . . If, in spite of knowing this, we rely on Western ways of thought, even in teaching the Islamic sciences, it will be an unforgiveable blindness on our part."[32] There is therefore little room in his way of thinking to consider cultural borrowing from the West, though he thought it was permissible to learn sciences from Western sources when they were the only ones available. He agreed with the *salafiyya* thinkers that the first *umma* was the proper model for contemporary Islamic reconstruction, but he was implicitly at odds with them over the use of elements of Western theory and practice in that reconstruction. Among other things, his position in this regard led him to reject completely the doctrine of nationalism as inherently foreign to Islam: "The homeland of the Muslim . . . is not a piece of land; the nationality of the Muslim . . . is not the nationality determined by a government; the family of the Muslim . . . is not blood relationships; the flag of the Muslim . . . is not the flag of a country."[33]

Sayyid Qutb's interpretation of the Islamic revival added an important dimension to neofundamentalist ideology. His general rejection of the West and of Islamic societies as presently constituted, his refusal even to consider any kind of compromise with non-Islamic cultures and lifestyles, and his declaration of *jihad* against all *jahili* systems everywhere became major elements in the developing militant outlook. Many of his ideas are reflected in the writings of Ayatollah Khomeini, for example. One of his most articulate statements on the modern Islamic mission became the conceptual framework of the purist version of Islamic resurgence: "The foremost duty of Islam in this world is to depose jahiliyya from the leadership of man, and to take the leadership into its own hands and to enforce the particular way of life which is its permanent feature."[34]

An equally important aspect of Sayyid Qutb's intellectual legacy was that it overlooked the implications of the extent to which Islamic civilization represents a composite of diverse cultures adapted to the Islamic world view. Though he was aware that Islam and the West had certain cultural links, he could not deal with the fact that these stem from a common heritage, especially the philosophical and scientific traditions of classical Greece. Anxious to prove that the West is indebted to Islam for many of its own accomplishments, he made a case for the Islamic origins of European science: "One ought to remember the fact that the experimental method, which is the dynamic spirit of modern Europe's industrial culture, did not originate in Europe but originated in the Islamic universities of Andalusia and of the East."[35]

The narrowness of this interpretation helped to create a barrier in neofundamentalist thought to the conditional cultural exchange with the West found in the doctrines of the earlier Islamic modernists. Stereotyped political formulas and rigid generalizations consequently became characteristic of resurgence ideologies and precluded any genuine attempt to reexamine Islam in terms of its humanist dimensions. Qutb was not the only person responsible for this, but he was among those principally responsible.

The world view of Islamic resurgence has been elaborated by various other thinkers, leaders, and groups. Hasan al-Banna laid the foundation, and people like Sayyid Qutb added new ideas. Another contributor was Muhammad Jalal Kishk, whose thought was carefully analyzed by Fouad Ajami in his book, *The Arab Predicament*.[36] Kishk was a maverick Egyptian intellectual and writer with strong Muslim Brotherhood affinities. He saw the conflict between Islam and the West as essentially cultural, and indeed he understood world history as a struggle among competing cultures for ascendancy. Physical imperialism is actually a transitory phenomenon, but the permeation of Egypt and other Islamic countries by Western culture is a far more pernicious development. What contemporary Muslims do not realize, Kishk maintained, is that the West has managed to convince them that its own "cosmopolitanism" is superior and that Islamic tradition is obsolete. But, he insists, this deception has undermined the fabric of Muslim society by fostering a sense of inferiority and encouraging exploitation and inequity.

Kishk, like Hasan al-Banna and Sayyid Qutb, took particular issue with the Western concept of nationalism, by which so many Arab intellectuals had been seduced. In reality, it was a kind of Trojan horse, used by the West to keep the Arab world divided. Traditional Islam had been based on a universalism that produced multinational and ethnically heterogeneous empires. But when modern nationalism took root in the Middle East, particularism and regionalism became dominant and destroyed the unity of the area to such an extent that the West could easily establish and maintain control in one way or another. Whereas the spirit of the Islamic past was *jihad*, a source of strength, the spirit of the Islamic present is imitation of the West, the basic source of its vulnerability. What Muslims have to do, therefore, is to reaffirm their own culture and establish a legitimate Islamic sociopolitical order.

Though isolated as an individual, Kishk's ideas have made some impact on the development of neofundamentalist ideology. He added a degree of intellectualism to the formulation of some of the component concepts, but despite the pertinence of his arguments he is often involved in generalizations and questionable interpretations of history. His most important shortcoming, however, is his inability to look at Islam in its totality, examining its various dimensions, its triumphs, and its failures. His approach is defensive and apologetic rather than analytical and objective. It therefore lacks the flexibility and imaginativeness to develop a comprehensive reexamination of the Islamic tradition in order to revitalize the elements most appropriate to the conditions and needs of contemporary Muslim societies.

Another Kishk who played an important role in the resurgence movement in Egypt was Sheikh Abdul Hamid Kishk, a dramatic activist known for his fiery Friday sermons.[37] Using a combination of high classical Arabic and colloquial Egyptian, he drew his large audiences into an Islamic way of thinking that is critical of the secular nationalist order and its subtle infiltration of the religious institution. This popularization of a basic neofundamentalist idea—the purification of Muslim societies contaminated by Westernization—has helped prepare millions for the message of Islamic resurgence; Sheikh Kishk's sermons have been carried by the media, pamphlets, and cassettes into homes throughout the Middle East. Though not sympathetic with the violent splinter groups that broke off from the Muslim Brotherhood, Sheikh Kishk has instilled in many an anti-establishment frame of mind, a countersociety mentality, which has revolutionary implications.

By the early 1940s, the Society of Muslim Brothers had become a significant and active political force in Egypt. This time also marked the beginning of a rather turbulent period in that country's history. The society was destined to have heated encounters because of its marked opposition to the status quo and to secularism and nationalism. Hasan al-Banna had anticipated a stage of "execution" when the brotherhood would seek to implement its doctrines and begin the process of re-Islamization. In preparation for this, he had based the organization of the society on closely knit cadres, held together by a supervisory authority.[38]

The basic unit was an activist cell known as the "family" (*usra*), and at the end of 1942 Hasan al-Banna established a special paramilitary body commonly referred to as the Secret Apparatus (al-Jihaz al-Sirri). The function of this organization was to protect the society from the police and political adversaries and eventually to initiate the *jihad* and the re-Islamization process. In 1945, the hierarchical structure was formalized. Leadership was invested in a general guide (al-Murshid al-Am), a position initially held by Hasan al-Banna. He was assisted in his duties by a General Guidance Council (Maktab al-Irshad al-Am) and a Consultative Assembly (al-Hayat al-Tasisiyya). A rather elaborate support system was set up at lower levels.

The combination of this type of revolutionary organizational structure and an ideology that called for *jihad* against the status quo and designated secularism and nationalism as its principal enemies set the stage for an ultimate clash between the Society of Muslim Brothers and the other political forces in Egypt. Though King Faruq befriended the brotherhood briefly in an attempt to counter the role of the Wafd party, this alliance finally gave way to mutual animosity, and the society was dissolved by the government on December 8, 1948. Three weeks later, Prime Minister Nuqrashi Pasha was assassinated by a Muslim brother, and police gunned down Hasan al-Banna on February 12, 1949, in retaliation.

The society was reinstated in September 1951. Now under the leadership of Hasan Ismail al-Hudaybi, the brotherhood established contact with the Free Officers, who were plotting the overthrow of the government. After the coup of July 1952, the relationship continued in a tenuous fashion and then began to deteriorate. The sharp difference between the secular nationalist ideology of the Free Officers and the Islamic neofundamentalism of the society led to a confrontation that ended in the attempted assassination of Abdul Nasser on October 26, 1954. This action was followed by the arrest of thousands of Muslim brothers and the execution of six. Because of the popularity of the regime, the society came into general disfavor in Egypt.

Further friction developed between the Muslim Brotherhood and the Nasser government in the mid-1960s. Thousands more of the brethren were arrested and put on trial. Al-Hudaybi, who was serving a life sentence, was released in 1966 but then arrested again and sentenced to another term. He died in prison the same year. Sayyid Qutb was released from prison in 1964, having been incarcerated for ten years. But upon publication of a controversial book, he was arrested again in 1965 and was executed the following year. The society came to enjoy far better relations with the government in the 1970s, a topic discussed in Chapter 5.

The Muslim Brotherhood, despite its adversities, played a dominant role in the emergence and ideology of militant neofundamentalist Islamic movements in the second half of the twentieth century. It took the ideas of the largely intellectual and politically quiet *salafiyya* movement and converted them into an activist revolutionary ideology designed to galvanize the masses of Egypt into the vanguard of a future Islamic state. Its purpose was "to redefine the past in terms meaningful for the present"[39] and to inaugurate a process of re-Islamization through *jihad*. It considered the established clerical class, or *ulama*, to be totally incapable of accomplishing such a task because of its subservience to the ruling elite and its hypocrisy. It therefore designated itself as the herald of the new order. Its enemies were the West and those in Egypt and the rest of the Muslim world that had allowed itself to come under the influence of Western culture. The brotherhood was particularly adamant in its opposition to secular nationalism, which it regarded as a purely Western concept entirely alien to Islamic universalism and a source of divisiveness in the Middle East. It therefore fired the opening shot in the war between Islamic resurgence and the doctrine of nationalism. But it also reduced the quest for reform to a largely political issue, severely restricting the exploration of other more constructive avenues of change.

Islamic resurgence in Iran emerged in the context of the series of revolutionary upheavals that began with the popular opposition to Nasir al-Din Shah's concessions to the British in the late nineteenth century. The Shiite clergy played a major role in all the movements of the past one hundred years to check the power of the throne and thus became a permanent part of opposition politics in Iran. There have been three distinct grass-roots movements against the established authority since the 1870s. The first began with the protest against the Reuter concession of 1872 and the granting of a monopoly over the tobacco industry to Great Britain in 1890. Then the shah himself was assassinated in 1896, and by the end of 1904 a revolution of sorts began to take shape. This movement culminated in the reluctant agreement of the shah to promulgate a constitution in 1906. Though the liberalized system lasted only a few years, it marked the beginning of political change in Iran.

The events of 1921–1925, which resulted in the establishment of a new dynasty by Reza Pahlevi, represented a coup d'etat rather than a revolution. But the country was set on a new course in which the dominant themes were secularization, Westernization, and state-sponsored nationalism. In 1951, however, another revolutionary wave engulfed Iran, and Muhammad Reza Pahlevi was forced to appoint Musaddiq as prime minister and grant effective power to the National front. Like the earlier upheaval, this shift in political control was short lived and lasted just over two years. The last of the three revolutionary movements, by far the most dramatic, began in 1978 and led to the establishment of the Islamic Republic of Iran.

All these revolutions sprang from a popular base and involved a combination of secular and Islamic forces. The significant difference is that the secular wing was dominant in the first two, whereas the Islamic militants gained the upper hand in the last. Because Shiite Islam is particularly intolerant of anything suggesting political misrule or illegitimacy, the clerical class in Iran was more involved in public affairs and less passive than the *ulama* in Sunni countries. The *mullahs* and merchants participated together in the confrontation with the government in 1906. Again in 1951, the religious element constituted part of the National front. In both cases, however, there was evidence of disagreement between the Muslim activists and the secular revolutionaries as to goals and ultimate values. The former sought the Islamization of the political system, whereas the latter were primarily interested in liberalization along Western democratic lines.

This underlying conflict gradually drifted to the surface during the reign of the Pahlevis. Reza Shah had sharply curtailed the role and influlence of the *mullahs*, treating them at times with contempt. His pronounced secularism was not, however, an issue with that segment of the population that was rapidly moving toward Westernization, principally the urban middle and upper middle classes.

The exclusion of the clerical elements from the modernization process led those inclined toward Islamic activism to organize underground. The first of these secret groups was Fidaiyan-i Islam (Devotees of Islam), founded by Sayyid Mujtaba Navvab Safavi (1923–1956) after the accession of Muhammad Reza Shah in the 1940s.[40] The organization had contacts with the Muslim Brotherhood in Egypt and was strongly influenced by the ideology of Hasan al-Banna and Sayyid Qutb. Its members did not come from the religious leadership, and they remained a small contingent of young radicals dedicated to violent activism. They did, however, have the support of some of the higher clergy, and Ayatollah Khomeini admired Navvab Safavi and was closely associated with him.[41] Ayatollah Sadiq Khalkhali, who became the leading spokesperson of Fidaiyan-i Islam following the execution of Navvab Safavi in 1956, rose to a position of prominence in the Islamic regime of Ayatollah Khomeini. The organization carried out a number of assassinations between 1945 and 1963 but was mostly underground from 1951 until it emerged again in 1979.

By 1960, Muhammad Reza Shah had begun to consolidate his power. This evoked a negative response from both the old National front secularists and the clerical class. The White Revolution represented in part a move by the shah to form a tacit alliance with the peasantry while preventing the middle classes and the *mullahs* from playing a substantial role in the political process. But the aspect of the White Revolution that was unacceptable to the secular liberals was that the shah attempted to carry it out by fiat rather than through normal parliamentary channels. The clerics, on the other hand, were adamantly opposed to land reform and also to the shah's program of female emancipation, both of which they considered contrary to Islamic law.

In January 1962, a major riot broke out at Teheran University—the first symptom of what was to prove a growing tide of unrest.[42] The police and army brutally suppressed the uprising, and the shah dealt similarly with subsequent incidents of mass opposition. During the following months, Ayatollah Ruhollah Musavi Khomeini became the most outspoken senior cleric to take issue on Islamic grounds with the White Revolution and the emancipation of women. He was subsequently arrested at the holy city of Qum on the anniversary of Imam Hussein's martyrdom in early June 1963, in reaction to which demonstrations broke out in Teheran, Shiraz, Kashan, Mashhad, and Qum.[43] Once again, the police handled the protest with violence, and hundreds or more of the demonstrators were killed. Some of the students in Qum were hurled from the roof of the seminary to their deaths. On November 4, 1964,

Khomeini was exiled to Turkey but soon moved to the Iraqi holy city of Najaf, where he remained until 1978. During this period, he managed to create an image of himself as the titular leader of the opposition to the shah.

These events in the early 1960s were the beginning of the revolution that swept the shah from power in 1978–1979. But the only common denominator in this revolution was opposition to the shah's increasingly autocratic and repressive regime. Aside from that, a complex debate began to develop in the formative years as to Iran's future political and cultural direction. There was not only the basic division between the secular and Islamic wings of the movement but a variety of disagreements within each camp and a degree of overlapping.

The secular opposition, drawn largely from the urban middle classes, included the liberals and leaders of the old National front, such as Shahpur Baktiar, as well as various leftist organizations. These groups were not against the shah's modernization and Westernization policies, but they totally rejected his monopolization of power in Iran. Those to the right of center looked to a democratic parliamentary system of government; those to the left advocated a socialist or Marxist type of state.

The Islamic opposition was made up of two distinct schools—the moderates and the militant neofundamentalists.[44] The moderates, led by such leaders of the Iranian Shiite religious establishment as Ayatollahs Sayyid Muhammad Kazem Shariatmadari, Sayyid Mahmud Taleghani, Bahaeddin Mahallati, and Abdullah Shirzi-Qumi, Sheikh Ali Tehrani, and others sought a restoration of Islamic values in the sociopolitical system but were more interested in liberalization than Islamization of the institutional structure. The devout and respected layman, Mehdi Bazargan, also adhered to this view. The militant clergy came under the leadership of Ayatollah Khomeini and other prominent clerics, including Muhammad Beheshti, Hussein Ali Montazeri, Ali Akbar Hashemi-Rafsanjani, Morteza Motahhari, Abdul Karim Musavi Ardabili, Muhammad Javad Bahonar, and Ali Khamenei. They advocated a purely Islamic state, dominated by the religious establishment and dedicated to comprehensive Islamization and the elimination of Western culture from Iranian life. They were totally opposed to any form of compromise and regarded their task as one of purification.

Ayatollah Shariatmadari, widely regarded as the most learned and senior of the Iranian *ulama* after the death of Ayatollah Borujerdi in 1961, became the leader of the moderate Islamic opposition in the 1960s and 1970s. He was not opposed to the idea of constitutional monarchy itself but thought that the shah had ignored the established right of the higher clergy to approve or veto legislation as mandated by Article III of the 1906 constitution and that he had in general transgressed the proper limits of his power. He later became an advocate of republican government, though he insisted that it did not necessarily have to be Islamic. He favored a liberal democratic system based on the rights of all segments of the population and a flexible and moderate application of the *sharia*. He opposed the idea of clerical control of the political process, especially if it assumed the form of an Islamic dictatorship.

Because of his warm personality and tolerant attitudes, even toward foreigners, Ayatollah Shariatmadari acquired a broad following among those who liked his consistent support for traditional Shiite positions, as well as among the liberals and moderate opponents of the shah's regime. Those alienated by the relatively rigid and uncompromising ideology of the militant Islamic activists found him an appealing symbol of the required liberal shift in Iranian politics.

Another important moderate leader was Ayatollah Sayyid Mahmud Taleghani, who became closely associated with Mehdi Bazargan when the two participated in Musaddiq's National front in the early 1950s. Taleghani was the most progressive of the Iranian higher clergy and helped to create a bridge between the more moderate enthusiasts of Islamic reform and secularists who were prepared to support doctrines of comprehensive political change expressed in the language of repoliticized Islam. Like Shariatmadari, he took a strong position against an authoritarian religious state and the assumption by the *ulama* of a dominant or overbearing role. He was particularly popular with the Islamic-oriented leftist organization, Mujahidin-i Khalq-i Iran (Jihadists of the Iranian People). Bazargan, who was mainly interested in stimulating a new awareness and appreciation of Islam in sociopolitical affairs, was a favorite of the conservatives and middle-class elements that were receptive to such a message. These personalities were particularly influential in popularizing a liberal interpretation of the Islamic revival in Iran. But the ideology they advocated was at variance with the doctrines of the militant faction.

The moderate Islamic reformers in Iran were close to the spirit and outlook of the earlier Islamic modernists. Though they were convinced that Islam had much to offer in reforming the existing institutions, they were also aware that the Western concept of representative democracy could help to promote more open sociopolitical systems in the Middle East. They were not afraid of cultural borrowing as such, recognizing implicitly that Islam itself was a composite of various traditions. They also fully understood that in certain respects Islamic institutions had to be adapted to the conditions and requirements of the modern age. They simply wanted to make their contemporaries conscious of the important role Islam could play in rebuilding Iran. But such a thoughtful and sober approach to change went relatively unheeded at a time of bitter disillusionment and agitation.

Ayatollah Khomeini established a clear position of leadership over the Islamic militants following his confrontation with the regime in 1963. His ideology is a version of the position developed by the Muslim Brotherhood in Egypt and the Fidaiyan-i Islam in Iran. Central to Khomeini's thought is a bipolar view of the world, reviving the old concept of an irreconcilable conflict between the "realm of Islam" (*dar al-Islam*) and the "realm of war" (*dar al-harb*). His symbolism also alludes to the struggle between the Shiite hero, Hussein, and the Umayyad caliph, Yazid. But all this imagery is projected onto the contemporary situation, with particular reference to the encounter between Islam and the West and the infusion of Western culture into Iran and other Middle Eastern countries.

For Khomeini, Iran's overriding problem is its "contamination" by the norms, customs, and institutions of Europe and the United States, which had led to various forms of degeneration, most importantly moral decay and the monopolization of power by the shah. Therefore, the only solution to the country's degraded condition was "purification." Khomeini considers himself Iran's "deliverer," a divinely ordained leader of a "Party of God" dedicated to carrying out a *jihad* against alien culture and the enemies of Islam. This self-image is borne out by the fact that after the revolution he allowed people to refer to him as the "imam." He insists that he interprets this title in the Sunni sense to mean simply a religious leader. But clearly many understand it in terms of Shiite tradition to mean the Mahdi, a forerunner of the return of the hidden Imam and the restoration of just Islamic rule. Ayatollah Shariatmadari warned Khomeini that he was flirting with blasphemy by not clearly denying any pretensions to such a role.[45]

Khomeini's doctrine of Islamic government is also close to heresy from a traditional perspective. The central idea, as developed in his *Islamic Government* (*Hukumat-i Islami*),[46] is that absolute authority should be vested in a senior member of the *ulama* who understands the contemporary situation and is an expert in Islamic law. Such a person was to be installed as the *faqih*, or jurist, and the political system over which he presided would be designated the *wilayat-i faqih* (state of the jurist). The granting of such dictatorial powers has no precedent in orthodox Shiite political theory, but Khomeini justifies it on the grounds that the Westernization process has gone so far that an autocratic Islamic theocracy is needed to reverse the trend.

Khomeini's Islamic republic was to be ruled by the clerical class. The *faqih*, who had the right to appoint all the key members of the juridical system and to approve and dismiss the president, would be supported by a parliament in which clerics and Islamic militants were dominant. He was also to be in command of the armed forces. With these powers, he would carry out a comprehensive purge of the country. All vestiges of Western culture were to be rooted out by draconian measures, and in general a militant posture was to be adopted toward the Western world itself and the corrupted elements within Iran. Democracy and Western concepts of human rights were really irrelevant. All that mattered was the eradication of the foreign culture that had infected Iran, with its antisocial cult of the individual, its youth culture based on jeans and pop music, its indulgence in alcohol, drugs, and sexual promiscuity, and its materialism.

Another aspect of Khomeini's political theory is that since God has already revealed his legislation to humankind in the form of the *sharia,* the main function of government is to enforce this law consistently and literally. Particularly important is the administration of Quranic punishments—including flogging, stoning, and amputation—in the purification process. The assumption in this argument is that the final product will be a utopian Islamic society in which such Western concepts as the balance of powers and the protection of individual rights will be rendered meaningless because complete and perfect justice will already have been established.

Ever since he became a prominent figure in the Islamic resurgence movement in Iran, Khomeini has taken particular issue with the doctrine of nationalism, in much the same way as have Hasan al-Banna and Sayyid Qutb. He regarded nationalism as an especially insidious extension of Western culture into Iran and the rest of the Middle East because it had captured so much of the popular imagination. But for Khomeini, it remained a form of *shirk,* or blasphemy, because it encouraged people to transfer their loyalty from Islam to the new institution of the secular nation-state. Khomeini's own family background contains an element of transnationality in that his grandfather took up residence in India.[47] This aspect helped to give him a universalist aura that many found appealing, especially in contrast to the shah's pronounced state-sponsored nationalism, so widely publicized by the celebration honoring the 2500th anniversary of Iranian monarchy in 1971. Once in power, Khomeini made clear his determination not to tolerate any of the minority nationalist movements in Iran, such as those among the Kurds and Baluchis. He took an unequivocal stand against particularism, though he was forced to make some allusions to Iranian patriotism in the Iran-Iraq war.

Finally, Khomeini has for over twenty years considered himself the natural and probably divinely appointed leader of the Islamic resurgence movement in Iran. He is the helper of the "unseen Imam" and also a *marja-i taqlid* (model for emulation). This self-image made it possible for him to engage in a variety of political maneuvers and machinations without any sense of transgression, because of the sanctity of his mission. He also consciously sought to export the revolution from Iran on behalf of the interests of the transnational Islamic *umma*. Just as the struggle to which he has dedicated himself is global in scope, so also is his role.

Khomeini's ideology is very much the same as that of other resurgence leaders. But his interpretation of Islam as an almost exclusively political doctrine is especially pronounced. This view, combined with the fact that he actually succeeded in coming to power in Iran, was a major setback for those who understood the need to emphasize the humanist dimension in the Islamic revival. The character of the regime may, however, paradoxically lead to a new appreciation of Islamic humanism.

Eclectic Doctrines

Particularly in Iran, a unique kind of political ideologue appeared on the scene in the 1970s. Mostly young and Western-educated, these people combined the ideas about revolutionary change they had learned in Europe with a broad range of Islamic symbolism and phraseology. In this sense, they should be properly regarded as the authors of eclectic doctrines rather than as examples of a new version of Islamic modernism. Certainly, they played an important role in popularizing the Islamic resurgence movement and in creating the vocabulary of the 1978–1979 revolution in Iran, though at the time they were not aware of significant differences between themselves and the clerical leaders of Islamic militancy in the country. The best known among them were Jalal Al-e Ahmad, Ali Shariati, and Abul Hasan Bani-Sadr.

Jalal Al-a Ahmad (1923–1969) developed and popularized the idea that Iranians had been profoundly alienated from their own heritage and cultural identity because of the intensive Westernization of the country over the preceding one hundred years or so.[48] His famous and widely read essay, "Westoxication," asserted that Iranians had been intoxicated by the bewitching qualities of Western culture and had lost all real sense of who they were. The only way out of this dilemma was a rediscovery of Islam. Jalal Al-e Ahmad therefore adhered to the Islamic opposition to the shah and advised his countrymen to do likewise. Though he never developed a comprehensive ideology, he created a receptiveness to the subsequently developed eclectic doctrines that combined Western-inspired revolutionism and Islamic neofundamentalism.

Ali Shariati (1933–1977) was by far the most important of the nonclerical but Islamic-oriented ideologues of the eclectic doctrine category.[49] He was one of the key personalities in the development of the ideas that became an integral part of the movement against the shah in Iran. Educated in France, he was strongly influenced by Louis Massignon, Frantz Fanon, and Jean-Paul Sartre. But he was also interested in reinterpreting the symbolism of Shiite Islam so that it could become an integral part of the antishah political ideology. Like most of those involved in devising eclectic doctrines to be used in the opposition movement, he sought to overcome the negative legacy passed on by centuries of corrupt Islam and to demonstrate the relevance of genuine Islam with respect to contemporary challenges.

Ali Shariati made a sharp distinction between the original Alid Shiism, which was revolutionary in character, and the Safavid Shiism, which became the state religion in Iran at the beginning of the sixteenth century and ultimately represented the interests of the establishment. In the former, he found all the needed symbols for modern Iranians to reconstruct their national life on the basis of their own culture rather than Western models. The martyrdom of Hussein was the perfect example of the noble Muslim who refused to accept unjust and illegitimate rule. Hussein's slogan was "Death is better than life under oppressors," and his sacrifice should not stimulate mourning so much as a determination by all who look to him for inspiration to fight for truth and justice. Similarly, the role of the ideal Muslim woman was portrayed in the life of Fatima, who was the Prophet's daughter, Ali's wife, and the mother of Hussein. She had provided support and encouragement to this dedicated family, which was entrusted with the preservation of all the best Islamic traditions.

Safavid Shiism, on the other hand, had lost all this symbolism. It became an instrument of state power and enslavement and was geared much more to perpetuating dynastic authority than to acting as guardian over the principles of justice. It was a formalized kind of Shiism that had lost touch with the substantive message of real Shiite doctrine. Ali Shariati felt that the Pahlevis represented the most recent form of Safavid Shiism because they gave priority to the institution of the monarchy over the precepts of Islam. Therefore, the revolutionary ideology of contemporary Iranians in their struggle against the shah should be fashioned on the model of Alid Shiism. They should derive their inspiration from this liberating force.

Ali Shariati also reinterpreted some of Islam's most fundamental concepts in such a way as to awaken the popular imagination, especially among students. The term *tawhid* (unity) was traditionally used with reference to the Islamic affirmation of the oneness of God. But Shariati maintained that it should also be understood to mean commitment to social action designed to promote the harmonious integration of Islamic society. He held that *jihad* was more than the struggle to spread Islam; it was the collective will of Muslims to accomplish good in the world as well. *Hajj* was not just the commemorative pilgrimage to Mecca but the evolution of man toward God.

Abul Hasan Bani-Sadr's ideological position is closely related to that of Ali Shariati. Also French educated, he sought to synthesize the doctrines of the Afro-Asian liberation movement with the Shiite symbolism developed by Shariati and others.[50] His political philosophy is based on an interpretation of *tawhid* that holds that sociopolitical unity precludes any form of monopolization of power. "In an Islamic government," he asserted, "belief must not be an instrument of government, but government must be an instrument of belief. And this necessitates that it is the belief that governs." He also envisioned an Islamic state in which "everyone is responsible for all; everyone is imam and guide of all." This notably liberal view of the Islamic revolutionary idea made Bani-Sadr a popular figure in Iran and helped win him a large majority of the vote in the presidential election after the overthrow of the shah. His association with Khomeini, however, was the main reason for the victory.

The degree to which the ideas of Ali Shariati and Abul Hasan Bani-Sadr were based on sound Islamic theology or are a reflection of concepts they had been exposed to in the West is a moot point. Much of the ideological content of the eclectic doctrines is unquestionably of Western origin. This fact does not in itself render them invalid. The real issue is whether or not they involved certain intrinsic contradictions. On the one hand they were liberal in character and reflect some of the humanism found in Islamic modernism; they were also very politically oriented and designed to recruit a following for the militant neofundamentalists. There is, however, an enormous difference between the outlook and political philosophy of Ayatollah Khomeini and the ideological commitments of Shariati and Bani-Sadr. Yet Bani-Sadr supported and worked with Khomeini, helping him to come to power. At a later date, he learned through bitter experience that a formidable gulf separated him and the resurgence leaders, an oversight that resulted naturally from his naïveté with regard to the realities of power politics and his partially contradictory ideological position.

This problem inherent in the eclectic doctrines aside, the thought of Ali Shariati had a profound impact on Iranian youth and the Iranian masses as their opposition to the shah gathered momentum. The young intelligentsia and revolutionaries were persuaded by his arguments to express their political aspirations in terms of Islamic symbols. He became a hero of the Mujahidin-i Khalq-i Iran, which also venerated Ayatollah Taleghani. This group, which ultimately came into violent confrontation with Khomeini, combined the revolutionary ideas of the European Left with the Islamic imagery developed by Shariati in establishing its program of political activism.

Shariati also exercised a strong influence on the common people in Iran through his use of vivid Shiite symbolism. The story of the martyrdom of Hussein had played a prominent role in the popular culture through the *taziyeh*, or passion plays, which depicted the lives of the great imams.[51] The collective psyche of the masses was attuned to the pronounced dualism of Shiite dogma, at the very least on an unconscious level. The lines between good and evil had been sharply drawn, from a Shiite perspective, in the early stages of Islamic political history. Muhammad, Ali, and Hussein were the principal heroes in the cosmic struggle of truth against idolatry, legitimacy against usurpation, and justice against tyranny. The *taziyeh* plays focused on this polar conflict and instilled in those who watched them a keen awareness of the ultimate importance of the eternal fight against the unjust ruler. There are also overtones of pre-Islamic Iranian Zoroastrianism in this dualism. In any event, Ali Shariati awakened the underlying sense of dedication to a perceived cause of justice in many of his own people at a time when alienation from the regime was pervasive and a revolutionary tide was gathering momentum.

The Islamic reconstructionist response to the sociopolitical crisis in the Middle East represents the attempt of Muslims to retrieve their own religious heritage and make it the foundation of a new public order. The aim of the renewal movement is extremely important because it relates directly to a dimension of the human condition frequently overlooked in an age when utility is deemed to have the highest priority. Yet Islamic revivalism in general has encountered difficulties in its endeavors to foster a rebuilding of society based on its own values.

The initial problem was the failure of Islamic modernism to make its own essentially synthetic doctrine a broadly based frame of reference for the diversified reform movement. The subsequent rise of secular nationalism as the dominant political theme eventually evoked another kind of Islamic reaction in the form of neofundamentalism. Though they enjoyed greater popular support, the resurgence organizations had a unidimensional approach to Islam that in most cases had little humanistic content and emphasized the importance of political solutions. Attempts to develop hybrid doctrines combining neofundamentalist principles and a number of other concepts of proper order proved to be chimerical in terms of implementation. The situation that finally emerged as Islamic resurgence became part of the political equation in the Middle East was one in which ideology became more an instrument in the struggle for power than a blueprint for genuine change in the future.

5

Ideology and the
Struggle for Power

The division of the reform movement in the Middle East into religious and secular wings had since the formative phase created a tension between the advocates of the two approaches. The conflict was minimal until World War I, but thereafter it assumed the proportions of an irreconcilable confrontation, which continues to manifest itself today as a struggle for power in particular countries and throughout the region.

The encounter took on hostile overtones when the secularists began to establish control and to diminish or terminate the role of Islam in the political process. A particularly sensitive point was the sometimes condescending attitude of the new nationalist regimes toward Islamic tradition and customs. But as nationalism lost some of its hold over the people, the militant neofundamentalists became equally disparaging of their secular adversaries. As the exchange reached a heated and often bitter level, however, the respective ideological formulas became less a matter of faith than a rationale for platforms in the political struggle, with appropriate shifts in position as the advantages in doing so became apparent.

The Arab World

In the Arab world, the confrontation between secular nationalism and militant Islamic neofundamentalism has been especially antagonistic in Egypt and Syria. During the Nasser years, the relationship between the strongly nationalist Egyptian regime and the Muslim Brotherhood was tenuous at best and openly hostile at worst. There were violent clashes in the mid-1950s and mid-1960s, following which the brotherhood was eclipsed. It reemerged during the following decade. The great majority of the people supported their charismatic leader as opposed to the Islamic militants. A major reason for this support was that Nasser's political philosophy, whether by design or inadvertently, represented a combination of nationalist objectives and Islamic symbolism. As Malcolm Kerr put it: "At its broadest and most significant level, Nasserism is a movement of social and political reform whose highly nationalistic and activist spirit and pragmatic approach to policy decisions tend to conceal an eclectic, yet very conventional, neo-Islamic intellectual attitude."[1]

The implicit synthesis of a revisionist secular nationalism, transregional pan-Arabism, and Islamic reform made Nasserism an extremely popular doctrine and effectively diminished the underlying appeal of Islamic neofundamentalism among various segments of the population. The liberalism of the first generation nationalists had been discredited because of its almost total Western orientation, its tendency to favor the interests of the upper strata of society, and its involvement in corrupt practices. Arab socialism, by contrast, restated secular nationalism in a revised framework attuned to the needs of the masses. It also had a degree of Islamic content, reflected in its specific designation as "Arab."[2]

The pan-Arab aspect of Nasserism was equally well received. It replaced the narrow regional outlook of the Wafd with a transregional Arab frame of reference that had Islamic overtones and stood in defiance of the artificial fragmentation of the Arab area by the colonial powers. Both doctrines, therefore, appeared to resolve the conflict between the need to modernize and the need to preserve a distinctly Arab and Islamic identity. They also helped to bridge the communication barrier between the Westernizing elite and the more traditional masses.

After the 1967 Arab-Israeli war, however, Nasserism began to decline in popularity, while the prevailing mood of self-examination stimulated a new interest in Islamic resurgence. This led to the revival of the Muslim Brotherhood and the appearance of more radical splinter groups in the early 1970s after Abdul Nasser's death. Sadat actually encouraged the brotherhood to assume a role in Egyptian politics. This approach was part of a broader tactic to undermine the Nasserite and leftist opposition by enhancing his own religious credentials and appealing to Islamic sentiment in the country.[3] Members of the society who had been exiled in 1954 and 1965–1966 were allowed to return, and Umar al-Tilmisani was permitted to revive the organization's main publication, *al-Dawa (The Call)*.

Though the Society of Muslim Brothers generally cooperated with Sadat in response to these gestures, the more militant splinter groups became increasingly hostile toward his regime. Two of the earliest splinter organizations appeared in 1971.[4] Munazzamat al-Tahrir al-Islami (Islamic Liberation organization), later known as Jamaat al-Faniyya al-Askari (Technical Military Academy group), was founded by a Palestinian named Salih Siriya. Shukri Mustafa, an Egyptian, established Jamaat al-

Muslimin (Society of Muslims), more commonly referred to as Takfir wa al-Hijra (Excommunication and Emigration, in the sense of figurative departure from an unbelieving society).[5] Both operated underground and were committed to overthrowing the government and setting up an Islamic state. In April 1974, the Islamic Liberation organization tried to initiate a coup by taking over the Technical Military Academy, an action that earned it the nickname of Technical Military Academy group. The attempt was unsuccessful, however, and Siriya was executed and others directly involved were given prison sentences.

Takfir wa al-Hijra was more cautious in its tactical revolutionary doctrine because it considered the entire society to be as contaminated by alien beliefs as the government was. But the food riots of January 1977 and the regime's subsequent harassment of all opposition groups gradually drew the organization into a confrontation with the authorities.[6] When the demand for the release of arrested Takfir wa al-Hijra members was denied, the group kidnapped the pro-Sadat former minister of religious endowments, Hussein al-Dhahabi, in July 1977. The government refused to back down and al-Dhahabi was executed by his captors. The Takfir wa al-Hijra leaders were then arrested and put on trial, resulting in the execution of Shukri Mustafa and the jailing of thirty-six.

The attempts to contain the activities of such radical Islamic organizations only stimulated their proliferation. R. Hrair Dekmejian identified twenty-nine neofundamentalist groups in Egypt, of which the most important are the Muslim Brotherhood, Jamaat al-Faniyya al-Askari, Takfir wa al-Hijra, and the more recently founded al-Jihad (Holy War) organization.[7] Despite Sadat's deference to Islam and the Muslim Brotherhood, most of those involved in the repoliticization of Islam took increasing exception to his policies. They were particularly disturbed by the rapprochement with the United States and the peace treaty concluded with Israel. They also opposed the *infitah* economic program, which seemed to benefit mainly the wealthier classes, and the only nominal liberalization of the political system. In March 1979, university students in Asyut, the center of the Jihad organization, staged an anti-Sadat demonstration that was disbanded by the police and followed by the illegalization of political activity on campuses.

Sadat was now in deep conflict with neofundamentalism in general, and even the formerly cooperative Muslim Brotherhood criticized him severely in *al-Dawa* and its other major publication, *al-Itisam* (*Perseverance*). In September 1981, these publications were banned and al-Tilmisani was placed under arrest. Members of the Jihad organization were also detained. Within this climate of hostility between Sadat and the Islamic opposition members of Jihad who had infiltrated the army assassinated the president on October 6, 1981. Following this action an open confrontation in Asyut developed between Jihad and the police and security forces amid widespread arrests of the organization's members.

The tension between the secular-nationalist order and Islamic neofundamentalism has eased somewhat under the presidency of Husni Mubarak. Though very firm in curtailing any violent action by the militants, he allowed them to express their views in the public media.[8] The genuine liberalization of the political system, a sterner attitude toward Israel, and attempts to repair relations with other Arab states also made Mubarak much more acceptable to the radical Islamic organizations than his predecessor. Though Mubarak has given these groups some freedom of movement, an enormous ideological gulf remains between them and the regime. The president's interest in promoting the Hussein-Arafat peace initiative, for example, could not be well received in Islamic circles. Furthermore, there is little in common between the basically secular orientation of Egypt under Mubarak and the concept of an Islamic state as understood by those involved in the Islamic resurgence movement.

The uneasy truce effected in the secular-Islamic dichotomy can be broken at any moment. The popularity of the neofundamentalist political doctrine increases as the Egyptian populace perceives a greater and greater discrepancy in the way policy serves the interests of elite groups as opposed to those of the common people. The April 1987 Egyptian elections, widely reported to have been the most open in recent years, indicate the persistent popularity of the Islamic resurgence movement. The militant organizations are not, however, made up of lower class, proletarian revolutionaries. The members are predominantly from the middle and lower middle classes, often from rural backgrounds and recently urbanized.[9] They are also mostly young and highly educated, some 80 percent being enrolled in or graduated from urban colleges and universities. As highly motivated advocates of change endowed with these qualifications, they effectively represent the interests of the poorer masses of Egypt and easily assume a leadership role for most alienated segments of the population. Though their ideology is distinctly religious, they are often not extremely well versed in Islamic theological sciences and are primarily concerned with the kind of sociopolitical reconstruction that most underprivileged people feel would be more equitable.

Saad Eddin Ibrahim has summarized succinctly the psychopolitical climate of contemporary Egypt:

> Egyptians have engaged for a century in a quest for social justice, cultural authenticity, development, real independence from big powers, and closer integration in its Arab-Islamic spheres.

This quest has been frustrated time and again by their rulers and foreign powers alike. This is the heart of their crisis.[10]

Though there does not now seem to be any likelihood of a successful Islamic revolution in Egypt, such as occurred in Iran, the resurgence movement is bound to gather momentum if President Husni Mubarak and his successors fail to deal effectively with the crisis. The current situation in the country is basically a stalemate, compounded by a communication barrier, in which a secular regime representative of the cosmopolitan urban middle classes is trying to pacify or contain revolutionary tendencies, while an activist Islamic opposition defending the rights of the underprivileged plays the game by the established rules and waits for opportunities to enhance its position. In many respects, the two sides talk past each other and make little attempt to understand or consider the other's position. The secularists see no constructive role to be played by Islam, while the neofundamentalist militants are often so preoccupied with the politicization of their religion that they are unable to deal with the humanist dimensions of Islam, which would make them much more appealing to those in the society who distrust them. The myopia on both sides perpetuates the underlying conflict, but the tension between two antagonistic public philosophies increases as the issues of equity are left unresolved.

The Syrian branch of the Muslim Brotherhood was founded in Aleppo in 1935. It had close ties with the society in Egypt, though it remained independent. In 1944, its center shifted to Damascus, where its leader. Sheikh Mustafa al-Sibai of the Homs *ulama,* succeeded in bringing other Islamic resurgence groups under the wing of the brotherhood.[11] After the Syrian-Egyptian merger in 1958, the society was outlawed and al-Sibai died in prison in the early 1960s. The organization stayed underground after the dissolution of the United Arab Republic (UAR) in 1961, and its new leader, Isam al-Attar, took refuge in West Germany, from where he tried to direct its activities. After the Baath party came to power in 1963, the society and affiliated organizations were increasingly drawn into a bitter confrontation with the regime on ideological grounds, challenging its secular nationalism with the society's own diametrically opposed doctrine of Islamic government. The brotherhood declared a "jihad against the enemies of God"[12] at the outset and actively sought to unseat the new ruling elite.

The Islamist-secularist struggle in Syria assumed a marked intensity and extended beyond the confines of ideological conflict because of the dislocations in the sociopolitical structure introduced by the Baath.[13] The traditional dominance of the Sunnis, who constitute 70 percent of the population and of the urban middle and professional classes was gradually undermined by the Baath leadership, which recruited its backing in other sectors. Increasingly, they turned to minority sects, especially the Alawites, a heterodox Shiite denomination, and to the rural constituencies to fill their cadres and to occupy strategic positions in the military. This tactic was specifically designed to shift power away from the older elites and build support bases among other groups that had formerly played a minimal role in running the state. The secular and populist nature of the Baath's ideology was perfectly attuned to this methodology. The 12 percent Alawite community had the least stake in the old system and its members were easily drawn into the Baath cadres. The Christians (11 percent), Druze (3.4 percent), and Ismailis (1.6 percent) also appreciated the secularism of the new regime, which placed minority sects on equal footing and enabled them to play a much more active role in Syrian politics than previously. Since many of these groups were based in towns and villages, the Baath's support had a distinctly rural coloring.

The Sunni majority, the urban bourgeoisie, and the *ulama* were quickly alienated by this transformation of a political structure that had prevailed for centuries. These defenders of the old order therefore gradually developed a tacit alliance with the Islamic resurgence organizations, which challenged the Baath's claims to represent the common people and dismissed the government as a corrupt and irreligious minority regime. Though often not drawn to the doctrines of Islamic neofundamentalism, this largely urban, Sunni, and middle-class opposition regarded the Muslim Brotherhood and its affiliates as the natural open combatants in the struggle against the Baath. They supported them and sometimes joined in the armed confrontations.

The first encounter was in April 1964, when the very traditional Sunni community of Homs, encouraged by the Muslim Brotherhood, staged a revolt that was brutally suppressed by the authorities. When the ardent Baathist, Salah Jadid, came to power in February 1966, all forms of opposition met with harsh retribution, resulting in the departure of some from the country and the virtual isolation of the government.[14] Another power struggle within the Baath led to the accession of Hafiz al-Asad in November 1970. Pragmatic and moderate in disposition, al-Asad adopted more accommodating policies in an attempt to revive support for the regime.

Al-Asad's different approach was nevertheless unsuccessful in preventing the increasing radicalization of the Islamic resurgence movement. Intensely militant groups formed earlier were reactivated and began to play an important role in the confrontation with the Baath.[15] These included the Islamic Liberation party (Hizb al-Tahrir al-Islami), which was founded in Jordan in 1952 by Shaikh Taqi al-Din al-Nabhani and had spread to Syria, and Muhammad's Brigades (Kataib Muhammad), created by Marwan Hadid. A more dynamic group was formed in the 1970s as a splinter from the Muslim Brotherhood. Entitled the Combat Vanguard of the Jihadists (al-Talia al-Muqatila lil Mujahidin), it initially came under the leadership of Marwan Hadid until his death in prison in 1976. Salim Muhammad and Adnan Aqla subsequently headed the organization, but they also were taken into custody and were later replaced by Adnan Sadr al-Din, Ali Sadr al-Din Bayluni, and Said Hawi.

The Combat Vanguard became the most aggressive of the militant Islamic factions in the struggle against al-Asad in the late 1970s and early 1980s. Its ideology, however, is less dogmatic than that of most Islamic resurgence groups, and it is relatively liberal in its political orientation. While advocating an Islamic republic, it rejects the idea of clerical supremacy, assigns ultimate authority to a freely elected parliament, and opposes all forms of violation of private property. In this respect, it is particularly appealing to the gentry and urban middle class, which gave increasing financial assistnce to Islamic militants as the confrontation with the regime escalated in intensity.

Though al-Asad tried to soften the Alawite coloring of the regime and to strike a sectarian balance in appointments to reflect geographic distribution, he constantly faced mounting opposition. The constitution of 1973, of which he was the principal author, was extremely secular and did not establish Islam as the religion of the state. Though completely in accord with Baathist doctrine, this orientation was offensive to many Sunnis, and rioting broke out in Homs, Hama, and Aleppo. To calm the situation, al-Asad added an article specifying that the president had to be a Muslim and tried to promote an image of himself as personally devout. In terms of internal politics, however, he made a tactical error by intervening in the Lebanese civil war on the Christian side in 1976, evoking criticism from the Sunni community.

By 1979, al-Asad's encounter with the opposition had assumed violent dimensions. One June 16, a Sunni officer with accomplices at the Aleppo Artillery school gunned down sixty Alawite cadets to protest the overwhelming majority of Alawites enrolled in the institution. This event was the first of a series of episodes in which the government resorted to displays of sheer force and bloody retaliations to quell the opposition. In March 1980, the shops of Aleppo were closed as a gesture of support for the Muslim Brotherhood and other Islamic resurgence organizations. In response, the army took over the city on April 6 to demonstrate that the regime would not tolerate such forms of active resistance. The following October, several militant Islamic groups created a Syrian Islamic front, which formulated an anti-Baath platform in a combination of religious and liberal terms designed to win the support of secular and leftist elements predisposed against the regime.[16] The battle lines were now sharply drawn, and on April 25, 1981, an insurrection broke out in Hama. The army crushed the uprising with dispatch and executed scores of the insurgents in the presence of their families. The Islamic militants later retaliated by killing over a hundred of regime's troops, and a similar confrontation took place in Hama in February 1982.

Islamic resurgence has posed a dramatic challenge to the regime in Syria because it represents a much broader opposition and has succeeded in making its slogans the vocabulary of the anti-Asad movement. But it is not organically or ideologically tied to those elements that seek a restoration of the traditional sociopolitical structure, and the component organizations within the militant Islamic camp are not closely knit and lack an adequately coherent strategy to conduct a large-scale revolution.

Two other factors severely restrict the possibility of establishing an Islamic government in Syria. The first is that the country is heterogeneous in sectarian composition, despite its Sunni majority, and cannot easily be brought under the kind of theocratic regime that the Islamic resurgence groups ultimately prefer. Second, Syria has strong historic links to the Arab awakening, and though many take issue with Baathism in practice, Arab nationalism still remains a powerful force. The neofundamentalist-nationalist dichotomy is not an underlying polarity in terms of the majority. Rather, a sizable opposition has used Islamic resurgence as a vehicle through which to combat the Baathist state. In view of these particulars and the government's firm control of the military, an Islamic revolution seems a remote likelihood in the foreseeable future. Yet politicized Islam will remain part of the political equation as long as the Baath continues its monopolization of power. The most important question in the long run is whether those who seek political liberalization in Syria will, if and when they achieve their goals, be able to consider the use of a broader interpretation of Islam in the reconstruction of their society.

The struggle for power between established regimes and Islamic resurgence organizations in other parts of the Arab world has varied in accordance with domestic circumstances, and the issues are not always the same. In Iraq, neofundamentalism developed principally among the Shiite community, which constitutes at least 55 percent of the population and is concentrated among the underprivileged classes in the south. The first and still most important organization to emerge was the Hizb al-Dawa al-Islamiyya (Islamic Call party), which R. Hrair Dekmejian dated as early as the late 1950s under the leadership of the renowned *mujtahid*, Ayatollah Baqir al-Sadr.[17] Hanna Batatu, however, claimed that it was founded in the late 1960s, possibly by another prominent Shiite *marja-i taqlid*, Sayyid Muhsin al-Hakim al-Tabatabai and without any involvement on the part of Baqir al-Sadr.[18] In any event, there is little doubt that both *mujtahids* had a profound influence on the Dawa party. Certainly, Baqir al-Sadr's political ideology, which was close to that of Ayatollah Khomeini and may have played a role in the formulation of Iran's Islamic constitution, was the intellectual beginning of Islamic resurgence among Iraq's Shiites and the inspirational source of al-Dawa's doctrines.[19]

As in Syria, the neofundamentalist movement in Iraq has taken particular exception to the secular nationalism, minority sectarian composition (in this case Sunni), and authoritarian character of the Baathist regime. The confrontation gathered intensity after the accession to power of Hasan al-Bakr and Saddam Hussein in 1968. In 1974, protest demonstrations against the government erupted during the commemoration of Imam Hussein's martyrdom. The authorities suppressed the outburst, arrested some of those involved, and executed five Dawa members. During the Shiite Muharram observances in 1977, rioting in Najaf and Karbala to protest interference by the military led to many arrests and subsequent imprisonment and executions. On the same occasion in 1979, a demonstration calling for an Islamic government brought about the arrest of Baqir al-Sadr, which was followed by more rioting and strong punitive measures by the authorities. These actions created some division within the Baath party over their intensity. Saddam Hussein, who had become president in July 1979, conducted a purge of the party at this time and tightened his political control of the country. He was determined to prevent the Shiite militant movement from challenging his leadership and had Baqir al-Sadr tried for treason after he had expressed support for the Iranian revolution and openly defied Baathist rule. The respected ayatollah was executed in April 1980.

Operating with the relatively narrow support base of Iraq's twenty percent Arab (as opposed to Kurdish) Sunni minority and the clique from the Takrit region that is predominant in the Baath, Saddam Hussein has sought to contain the neofundamentalist Shiite threat through a combination of forceful suppression and deference to Shiite interests, reflected in religious subsidies and active economic support for the sect's poorer communities.[20] Though numerous more militant Islamic resurgence organizations, such as the Mujahidin (Jihadists) and the Munazzamat al-Amal al-Islami (Organization for Islamic Hope), appeared in the late 1970s, the proliferation was symptomatic of factionalism in the movement rather than an escalating tide of opposition. Also, a majority of the Shiites have a strong sense of Arab identity and supported Saddam Hussein in the war against Iran.

The regime is therefore reasonably secure though its hold on power will alienate some elements that will tend to use Shiite neofundamentalist symbols in expressing their displeasure with the status quo. The Shiite majority and the pronounced repoliticization of Shiite Islam in recent years are therefore still part of the political scene in Iraq. Other factors that will play a role in shaping the course of events are the frustrations arising from the extended and unresolved war with Iran and the questions posed by the character and malpractices of the Khomeini regime. Also, the Baathist government has a lot to account for in terms of its own record and cannot continue to monopolize power indefinitely. In one way or another, the Islamic issue has to be raised in the quest for a more acceptable sociopolitical system. The unknown is what aspects of the Islamic tradition Iraqis will turn to as they try to accomplish this task.

Shiite militancy has also been active in Lebanon but within the context of the sectarian strife that has beset the country since 1975. The Shiites are the largest single religious community in Lebanon, but they have not enjoyed a proportionate share of power and influence, and many of them are from the underprivileged strata of society. Because of their heavy concentration in the south, they were often caught in the Israeli-Palestinian cross fire that has ravaged the area for over a decade with considerable loss of life and property.

Imam Musa al-Sadr, cousin of Muhammad Baqir al-Sadr and an Iranian *mujtahid* who had been a protégé of Ayatollah Khomeini and became the religious leader of the Lebanese Shiite community in 1960, worked actively to improve the lot of the underprivileged Shiites from his headquarters in Tyre.[21] When the civil war began, he created the organization Amal (Hope) to serve as the Shiite militia on the Muslim-Druze-Palestinian side. After al-Sadr's mysterious disappearance in Libya in 1978, Nabih al-Barri became head of Amal and of much of the Shiite community.

As the civil war degenerated into an anarchic conflagration in which each sect was against every other and former allies became enemies, more radical Shiite organizations appeared. Two of the most active were Hizb Allah (Party of God), under the nominal leadership of Sheikh Muhammad Hussein Fadlallah, and Hussein al-Musawi's Islamic Amal, both founded after the Israeli invasion of Lebanon in 1982.[22] These organizations became involved in protecting Shiites from other sects and Palestinians and in launching devastating attacks on U.S. and French installations in particular. Supported by Iran, they share Khomeini's view of the world and form part of an interrelated, international Shiite activist network. Given the extremely heterogeneous nature of Lebanese society, however, they seem to have no clear strategy for establishing an Islamic government. Their major actions seem to be directing unexpected terrorist strikes to keep local adversaries and foreign intruders off balance.

Though the Kingdom of Saudi Arabia is itself a fundamentalist Islamic state, it is opposed from within by radical neofundamentalist forces, as well as by some secular and leftist groups. Islamic activism, however, poses a greater threat. As James Bill pointed out, the confrontation is between populist Islam (*al-Islam al-shabi*) and establishment Islam (*al-Islam al-rasmi*).[23]

The Saudi kingdom was the product of a long formative phase, which began with an alliance between the Saud family of Dariyya (near Riyadh) and the fundamentalist religious leader, Sheikh Muhammad Ibn Abdul Wahhab, in the eighteenth century. But the real architect of present-day Saudi Arabia was Abdul Aziz Ibn Saud, who between 1902 and 1932 assembled the various components of the new kingdom under his own rule, initially with the help of tribal fundamentalists known as the Ikhwan (Brethren). In the 1920s, the Ikhwan began to challenge Ibn Saud's authority, but in 1929 he defeated them in the Battle of Sabala and consolidated his power. This episode foreshadowed the later encounter between populist Islam and establishment Islam.

After Ibn Saud's death in 1953, Saudi Arabia entered a continuing period of modernization and change that brought it out of isolation and effected substantive alterations in lifestyle and sociopolitical interaction. By the 1960s, opposition began to appear as a reaction to some of the regime's Westernizing tendencies, its cordiality with the United States, and its firm hold on power as a dynastic elite. The Ikhwan resurfaced in a new form as a neofundamentalist adversary of the government. The assassination of King Faisal in 1975 was reportedly an act of retaliation for the killing two years earlier of the revived Ikhwan's leader.[24]

The seizure of the Grand Mosque in Mecca on November 20, 1979, was a far more significant event. Carried out by the Ikhwan under the leadership of Juhayman al-Utayba, it involved mainly native Sunnis from tribes that had played the major role in the earlier Ikhwan movement.[25] Though the authorities eventually brought the situation under control, the incident raised questions concerning the regime's legitimacy. The drama surrounding the takeover of Islam's holiest shrine, the proclamation by one of the leaders that he was the Mahdi, and the accusations of the insurgents that the rulers of the country were corrupt, inept, and insensitive to the needs of the poor demonstrated that the government was opposed by some on the basis of its alleged failure to live up to Islamic values. Though these events probably do not foreshadow a revolutionary uprising, they do underline the differences that separate populist from establishment Islam. This distinction is important at a time when the status quo in the Middle East is being challenged, especially by the doctrines and slogans of neofundamentalist Islamic resurgence. The struggle for power throughout the area has acquired a new focus that has made differing interpretations of Islam as important an issue as the old dispute between secularists and Islamists.

Islamic militancy is less pronounced in the Gulf sheikhdoms, though it does exist as a reaction among some Sunnis to dynastic monopolization of political and economic power, and among Shiites to the predominantly Sunni affiliation of the ruling elites despite the heterogeneous sectarian composition of the local populations.[26] The existence of a sizable non-indigenous labor force and striking disparities in wealth also contribute to the growth of Islamic neofundamentalism. The Iranian regime has actively sought to promote Islamic revolutionary movements in the Arab states of the Gulf, especially in Bahrain with its Shiite majority. But an attempted coup in Bahrain in December 1981 was effectively checked, and similar episodes have not occurred elsewhere. Though Islamic resurgence is part of the political equation in the Gulf sheikhdoms, the relatively flexible and benign style of the respective regimes helps to minimize any tendencies toward insurrection against the established order.

Islamic resurgence has only indirectly affected politics in the Maghreb, and no imposing militant organization has been formed to challenge the nationalist governments. The independence movements against French colonial rule incorporated a degree of Islamic content in their otherwise nationalist ideologies, but this inclusion was largely to add emphasis to the distinct cultural identity they were trying to emancipate. The governments that were formed after liberation were mostly secular, and even the Moroccan king, Muhammad V, promoted an image of himself as both a religious leader and head of a modern state. Algeria and Tunisia used very pronounced Western models for their political systems. All these regimes professed Islam as a reformist frame of reference rather than as the basis of a political order, and this position was widely accepted. But the fact that they were all firmly entrenched and have remained in power for more than a generation eventually led to some forms of dissent and the use of Islamic terminology to express it—an imitation of a growing trend throughout much of the Islamic world.

According to Jean-Claude Vatin, the emergence of Islam as a new dimension in Maghrebi politics has led to a widespread use of Islamic symbols as an alternate political language in communications between ruling elites and their constituents.[27] If this inclusion in certain respects represents a superficial use of Islam in public dialogue, a far more profound investigation of Islam's relevance to current sociopolitical issues is being carried on by a few intellectuals. They all maintain an extremely low profile, and they have had very little impact because of the sensitivity surrounding what they have to say.

Perhaps the most prominent personality in this group is the Algerian scholar, Mohammed Arkoun. Troubled by what he sees as the inadequacies of both the secular nationalists and the Islamic neofundamentalists in addressing the task of sociopolitical reconstruction in the Middle East, Arkoun advocates the rediscovery of the real traditions embodied in historical Islam and a balanced approach to the establishment of a constructive relationship between Muslim societies and the outside world. He finds current attempts at Islamic revival impoverished in this respect: "Contemporary Islamic thinking disposes of neither the intellectual equipment nor the social-cultural cadres essential for thinking through not only the relations of Muslims to their own history, but their relation to the outer world and to its history."[28] Arkoun's ideas on this important subject will be further examined in Chapter 7.

Though Islamic resurgence has been less pronounced in the Maghreb than in other parts of the Arab world, there have been some marginal efforts to launch militant opposition movements, and a new interest exists in Islamic identity and practice particularly among the young. The example of the repoliticization of Islam in other countries has also exercised some influence. But whatever Islamic revivalism is present in the Maghreb is basically moderate and adapted to the interests and inclinations of the people themselves.

Libya, considered to be part of greater Maghreb, is a special case. The Islamism of Colonel Muammar Qaddhafi is unique and largely the product of its author. Though Qaddhafi projects an image of himself as an Islamic reformer, his political philosophy is far more strongly influenced by nationalism and other Western ideologies than by any interpretation of Islam.[29] It is actually based on a mixture of various doctrines within a nominally Islamic framework. None of the component themes is clearly worked out, and they are not brought together cohesively, producing a somewhat incoherent set of principles. The combination of an obscurantist platform and Qaddhafi's erratic personality and impulsive decisionmaking has alienated Islamic revivalists and secularists alike in other Middle Eastern countries. The Libyan leader must therefore be classified as a maverick and something of an anomaly in the context of the political changes currently unfolding in the area.

The ideological dispute between secular nationalism and militant Islamic neofundamentalism has become a key element in the struggle for power in the Arab world. Those segments of society having little stake in the status quo and disillusioned by the unfulfilled promises, monpolization of power, and corruption of the nationalist regimes have been attracted to the ideology and political activism of the Islamic militants. Their doctrines have provided the framework and vocabulary of opposition, and their component groups have mobilized and directed the struggle of the disaffected populace. But the resurgence movement lacks a cohesive organizational structure and a coherent revolutionary strategy. Its image has also been tarnished to some degree by the malpractices of the Islamic regime in Iran, which are as unappealing as those of some secular governments.

Though many in the Arab world are still attached to the doctrine of nationalism—a basic ingredient of the Arab awakening and the inspiration of the anticolonialist liberation movement—most nationalist regimes have been at least partially discredited. Thus the majority of people are torn between competing ideologies that have become platforms in the struggle for power more than genuine blueprints for sociopolitical reconstruction. The principal need today is a more mature and equitable understanding of nationalism and a more comprehensive and historically oriented interpretation of Islam.

Iran

The struggle for power in Iran was from its beginning in the 1960s a multisided confrontation of competing camps with diverse political beliefs. Differences were initially concealed by the common opposition to the shah, which created the appearance of a relatively uncomplicated battle between those for and those against the government. In the earlier revolutionary movements of 1904–1911 and 1951–1953, the antiregime forces had been very heterogeneous, which was also the case in the later period. There was therefore an implicit rivalry among the respective ideologies beneath the surface. The determining factor in the ensuing power game was the ability of the advocates of the different reform doctrines to win broad support for their particular form of opposition as the most effective way of overthrowing the shah.

An important element in this fluid political situation was the existence in Iran of what Nikki Keddie called the "two cultures" syndrome.[30] Though class differences had existed in earlier periods of the country's history, all levels of society had shared the same basic culture. During the Pahlevi era, however, a dichotomy developed between the increasingly European outlook of the Westernized elites and the popular culture of the masses. This cleavage in the social fabric, so common in most Third World countries, played a key role in deciding the drift of Iranian opposition politics. Since Islamic symbols were an integral part of the popular culture, the vocabulary and position of the neofundamentalists had the significant advantage of broad appeal among the alienated grass-roots populace.

A corollary of this particular aspect of the political equation was the anti-Western trend in the country. Despite the European orientation of the urban middle classes, the modernizing policies of the Pahlevi regime had acquired a negative stigma. Everything the shah did to emphasize the progressive character of Western-style innovations or to reinforce the sense of Iranian national identity at the expense of the Islamic was not well received. The pronounced pre-Islamic symbolism reflected in the 1971 Persepolis celebration, for example, not only increased the disaffection of the masses but also inclined those of the Westernized elites who opposed the autocratic system to reidentify with Islam.

As the movement to remove the shah gathered momentum in the 1970s, the Islamic approach to opposition gained popularity. As James Bill put it, "the Iranian people took refuge in religion and flocked to the mujtahids for social and political shelter. When these centers themselves became the targets of regime attack, the ulama decided to fight back to the end."[31] Each step the shah took to contain the influence of the Shiite establishment, however, only further ensured the Islamic character of the revolutionary trend.

At the time of the Persepolis celebration, the government closed a well-known meeting place in north Teheran where religious leaders and social critics such as Ali Shariati had expressed their views on the political situation in Iran.[32] This was the first of a series of attacks by the regime on a broad spectrum of Islamic-oriented dissenters, which heightened the level of confrontational tension. In June 1975—exactly twelve years after the uprising over Khomeini's arrest—another mass demonstration at Qum was brutally suppressed by the police.[33] By 1978, Khomeini was orchestrating protests all over the country, resulting in some bloody encounters with the authorities.[34] At this point, the ayatollah established his titular leadership of the ensuing revolution and maintained a powerful communication link with the Iranian people.

Many reasons lay behind the tilt toward the Islamic resurgence leadership of the antishah movement. One was the widespread feeling that the traditional balance between the ruling and religious institutions in Iran had been irreparably upset by the shah, creating an unacceptable dislocation in the political structure of the country.[35] Other issues included the curtailment of human rights and freedom of press, the repressive role of SAVAK (the shah's secret police), the concentration of wealth on the shah's aspiration to make Iran the dominant regional power in the Middle East and to enlarge his own personal fortune, and the closeness of the regime to the United States. Many also thought the government had far exceeded its constitutional prerogatives and was unable or unwilling to try to gratify the rising expectations of the people on various levels of society. Some thought the process of Westernization had gone too far.

Khomeini and the militant neofundamentalists had positions on all of these questions. These were often not, however, the same positions as those of other oppositionist groups. Indeed, a number of more moderate political leaders cautioned the ayatollah against the extremist character of some of his statements. Khomeini's tactic in this context was to emphasize the aspects of his platform with the widest appeal, leaving the more controversial topics, such as purification and re-Islamization, to be dealt with later. Unrelentingly, he castigated the shah, insisting that he was responsible for all the ills that had befallen Iran and that he was therefore the single most important issue. Indifference to traditional Iranian values, complicity in the designs of the United States, corruption, and exploitation of the Iranian people were his cardinal offenses, and he was held in contempt by most people throughout the country.

This uncompromising frontal attack on the shah and his regime had broad appeal, and sustained the momentum of the revolutionary tide. But it also kept the political differences among the oppositionist groups well disguised. The fervor of the antishah sentiment and the intensity of the demand for dramatic change enabled Khomeini to use ideology as an effective tool in his quest for power. Tailoring his arguments to the mentality and preferences of various audiences, he brought many who were inherently opposed to his way of thinking under his own aegis.

Khomeini's ultimately successful gambit was facilitated not only by the trend in the 1970s toward an Islamic expression of the opposition movement but also by the popularization of the eclectic doctrines, which articulated leftist and antiestablishment ideologies in the language of Shiite symbolism. Although Ali Shariati had already died before the initial phase of the revolution, his writings were instrumental in drawing large numbers of alienated students, youth, and working-class people into Khomeini's camp. Bani-Sadr and others who later became active in the revolution overlooked the differences between their own relatively liberal eclectic doctrines and Khomeini's political philosophy. They assisted the ayatollah in establishing his leadership and communication links with vast numbers of Iranians while he was still in exile. Unaware that they would eventually come into irreconcilable confrontation with the militant neofundamentalists, their naïveté made them unwitting accomplices of those advocating a revolutionary philosophy superficially similar to but actually in conflict with their own.

Other groups, such as the liberals and moderate Islamic reformers, had little success in using ideology to support their interpretations of the antishah movement. The old National front leaders lacked the ability to reach the masses, and only Shariatmadari and Taleghani among the Islamic moderates had significant, though mostly restricted, support. Therefore, Khomeini was never matched in political acumen by any of his adversaries. With a carefully devised game plan and most of the circumstances in his favor, he was able to subordinate the antishah movement to the neofundamentalist goal of building the foundations of an Islamic government under clerical control.

Though ideology was a motivating factor for the Khomeini camp, it was also a vehicle to be used in the struggle for power. Khomeini was a master at employing the slogans of Islamic resurgence to win over large segments of an angry and disaffected population. But this combination of idealism and pragmatic manipulation of a political doctrine to gain the advantage in a pluralistic rivalry was burdened with the inherent moral problem of justifying means for the sake of ends. It also virtually precluded any consideration of the nonpolitical aspects of Islam in attempts to reconstruct the Iranian sociopolitical system. Thus, though Khomeini did eventually come to power by the shrewd use of ideology as a tool, he inadvertently bequeathed a moral dilemma and a narrow perspective to those who later tried to implement the kind of government he advocated. He also did considerable damage to the idea of Islam as the basis of real justice and equity.

Turkey

Islamic resurgence as a countermovement to the secular nationalist order does not exist in Turkey in the same way as it does in Iran and the Arab world. This kind of ideological confrontation therefore plays a much smaller role in the struggle for power. When Mustafa Kemal Atatürk laid the institutional foundations of the Turkish Republic, he set the new state on a sharply defined course, one in which Islam was placed under government supervision and barred from playing any political role. However, Kemalism did not take into consideration the fact that though most Turks supported the doctrine of Turkish nationalism, a popular "folk" Islam remained a powerful social force in the country. The cosmopolitanism that developed from the pronounced secular tilt of the Kemalist system was far more evident among the urban elites and intelligentsia than in the majority of rural and lower class settings. It was therefore inevitable that at some point an Islamic revival of sorts would emerge in the sociopolitical fabric of Turkey.

The continuing efforts of Said Nursi and his followers to generate interest in an Islamic state were of no avail. But when the new Democratic party under Çelal Bayar and Adnan Menderes came to power in 1950, a number of concessions were made to those favoring a greater degree of Islamic content in Turkish life.[36] The Republican People's party had agreed to allow religious instruction in public schools the previous year, but the new government made such instruction mandatory unless parents specifically requested that their children not receive it. Other measures included the construction of mosques, the revival of Quranic broadcasts on the radio, and the reinstitution of the prayer call in Arabic. These gestures did not represent a retreat from Kemalism but rather a recognition that those involved in the political process could not ignore the fact that Islamic sentiment existed in Turkey.

Though the Democratic party was removed from power in 1960, the trend toward allowing Islam to play some role in the country did not come to an end. The 1961 constitution reaffirmed the principle of secularism, but the new Justice party (JP) of Suleiman Demirel, which replaced the now defunct Democratic party, continued to seek a compromise between the strongly Kemalist position of the military and the demands of the religious element in the country.[37] In 1970, Neçmettin Erbakan formed the National Order party as an Islamic splinter of the JP. The former was dissolved in 1971 for violating the constitutional ban on using religion for political purposes. But it was then reconstituted as the National Salvation party (NSP) in October 1972, and it won forty-eight seats in the parliamentary elections a year later.[38]

Erbakan claimed to represent a kind of Islamic neofundamentalism, calling for some limitations on alcohol consumption, prohibition of defamatory references to Islam, and increased religious education in public schools.[39] But despite his attempts to identify the NSP with neofundamentalism, he was a political opportunist and participated in coalition governments during the 1970s. The *ulama* did not play a significant role in the party, and in general it had only a superficial affinity with the militant Islamic resurgence organizations in other parts of the Middle East.[40] In the 1977 election, the NSP gained a lower percentage of the vote and lost much of its political leverage.

Despite the brevity of the NSP's influence, Islamic groups and ideologies were a factor in the Left-Right confrontations in Turkey during the turbulent 1970s. Troubled by the instability of the country and the sporadic outbursts of violence, some found consolation in a reidentification with Islam. Yet although an awareness of the situation was developing in Iran, few of the mostly Sunni Turks looked to figures like Khomeini for leadership and inspiration. Even the heterodox Shiite sect, the Alevis (Alawites), favored the secular orientation of the state because it protected them from the possibility of abuse by the Sunni majority.[41] Nevertheless, some Islamic themes had been injected into Turkish politics.

The military takeover under General Kenan Evren on September 12, 1980, helped restore stability to the country. All forms of radicalism, including Islamic neofundamentalism, were quickly harnessed, and a new political system, dubbed "disciplined democracy," was gradually constructed. But the military leadership was careful to show no hostility toward Islam and even expressed an interest in securing a place for Turkey in the international Muslim community.

The parliamentary election of November 1983 produced a majority for the Motherland party, and Turgut Özal became the prime minister. A moderate technocrat with a high level of sensitivity to all social currents in Turkey, Özal ran as an independent NSP candidate in 1977. He is known to be a devout Muslim whose political philosophy favors maintaining a reasonable degree of Islamic content within an essentially secular system. The platform of his party reads: "In preserving the values of secularism, we do not accept this as a restriction on the development of religious culture or the exercise of freedom of conscience, religious belief, or worship."[42] The victory of the Motherland party therefore reflects a renewed interest in Islam among the Turkish electorate, although religion was not a major theme in Özal's campaign. It is also significant that there is a rise in mosque attendance and in religious school enrollments. What seems to be most appealing to a large number of Turks is Özal's ability to reaffirm his commitment to Islam in a secular setting with which he is comfortable.

Turgut Özal also places a lot of emphasis on the importance of using Turkey's Islamic credentials to win support from other Muslim countries and to build bridges to Muslim peoples with whom the Turks have been in conflict in the past.[43] Particularly important in this regard are the attempts Turkey has been making for some time to bring about a rapprochement with the Arab world. While envisioning a leadership role for Turkey in the international Islamic community, Özal and many who support him also appreciate the benefits of reaffirming the country's Islamic identity at a time when militant neofundamentalism has become a political force in the Middle East. Given the instability of the area, this more balanced posture will certainly help to diminish the possibility of a revolutionary Islamic movement emerging in Turkey.

The Republic of Turkey is and will remain a secular nationalist state with a partially Islamic cultural heritage. Though the country has passed through difficult years, its people have not shown the kind of disenchantment with nationalism evident in other parts of the Middle East. The moderate return to Islam in Turkey is not a resurgence movement but an attempt to redress an imbalance that was an integral part of the Kemalist system. It represents a desire of the Turkish people to create a viable synthesis of values and identities in which Islam is allowed to play a part without excluding other elements of the national culture.

If the societies of the Middle East need to recover the better aspects of their own Islamic heritage without attempting to eliminate all traces of Western influence, Turkey conceivably could provide helpful guidelines for the kind of cultural synthesis that now seems necessary. Although the modernization process cannot be reversed, it has introduced a number of formidable problems relating to social integration and equity. Some attempts at revision within a secular framework have been partially successful, but most have been very disappointing. This failure has led to a largely incoherent search for Islamic remedies and alternatives. As these have been predominantly political in orientation, however, Islam has become more a platform in a power struggle than a basis for thoughtful self-examination and reflection on constructive change.

Turkey is one of the few countries in the Middle East in which the attempt to revive Islam has not been confrontational, but quiet, considered, and in conformity with the actual revisions that have become a permanent part of Turkish life. Perhaps only in such a climate of calm reconsideration can Islam be optimally useful in the task of reform and reconstruction. In this respect, Turkey may one day become an example for the other countries in the area.

When the ideologies of secular nationalism and Islamic resurgence became rationales for competing positions in a struggle for power, they deteriorated in substance and in usefulness. Principles were lost and issues were clouded. Former champions of justice became new despots. Moderation was reduced to a forgotten concept. Thousands were sacrificed for causes that had lost their meaning. Things got worse rather than better. Glib generalizations and vitriolic condemnations of adversaries ended up compounding the dilemmas they were supposed to resolve. The ideological confrontation in the Middle East has therefore only aggravated the breakdown of society in the area and left the quest for genuine reform in a state of disarray. Few took the time to analyze the dynamics of this impasse, but until this is done the situation will remain the same.

6

Profile of an Islamic Revolution

Political Rivalry in Revolutionary Iran

The revolution that gathered momentun in Iran throughout 1978 and finally overthrew the shah's regime in early 1979 represents the most dramatic confrontation between militant Islamic resurgence and various forms of liberalism in contemporary Middle East history. It was a classic encounter and will have a profound bearing on the secular-neofundamentalist dichotomy in this volatile region for decades to come. In winning the struggle for power, enabling them to establish an Islamic government, the neofundamentalists were actually putting their kind of Islamic revival on trial. They were providing an example of what their purist and literalist interpretation of Islamic government and culture entails with respect to human rights and freedom of expression. They were also exposing their inability to cope with the global cultural revolution because the eclectic humanist dimension of Islam was not part of their conceptual framework. Future generations in the Middle East will judge their doctrine on the basis of what it produced. But the question of how other interpretations of Islam might apply to sociopolitical reconstruction will remain unanswered.

As noted earlier, the opposition movement in Iran was highly diversified. It included two distinct clerical factions, advocates of eclectic doctrines combining Western radical concepts and Shiite symbolism, secular liberals, leftist groups, and parties representing the interests of the non-Persian nationalities. When the time was ripe in the late 1970s, the old regime fell almost automatically. The real struggle among the competing antishah factions was the only important issue at this point. In many respects, however, its outcome had already been decided by the rapport Khomeini had established with large numbers of the commonalty in Iran.

Beneath the complex structure of the organized opposition was an as yet not very clearly defined mass of underprivileged and unsophisticated people, some educated, for whom everything about the shah's political system and the Western culture it had introduced was both meaningless and oppressive. Included in this category were some nine million newly urbanized but discontented persons who had been uprooted from the rural areas by the land reform program of the White Revolution; some of the lower middle classes in the cities; and a large segment of the youth who had been divested of a sense of cultural identity and alienated by the old sociopolitical structure.[1] Though some of the latter were attracted by the parties of the Left, all these groups were vulnerable to the appeal of Islamic resurgence.

The most important development in the revolution was the recruitment of this disaffected sector of the population by Ayatollah Khomeini, though he initially had much broader support as the recognized titular leader of the antishah movement. When Khomeini established his reputation as the most articulate and uncompromising critic of the shah in 1962–1963, the trend among opponents of the regime had been to form some kind of working relationship with the clergy. This became a general pattern in the 1970s.

Aspects of Khomeini's past have a bearing on his rise to power and the character of the revolutionary government of which he was the major architect. In 1937, he had come into contact with the Muslim Brotherhood of Egypt through Sayyid Mujtaba Navvab Safavi, leader of the Iranian neofundamentalist organization, Fidaiyan-i Islam.[2] Both men shared the brotherhood's belief in the re-Islamization of the Middle East, though Navvab Safavi was almost exclusively an activist with a special bent for assassination, while Khomeini also had academic interests and aspirations. They complemented each other in these respects, however, occasionally working as an effective team. In 1942, for example, Khomeini published a pamphlet entitled *Key to the Secrets*, in which he attacked and called for the death of a popular anticlerical writer, Ahmad Kasravi. Navvab Safavi interpreted this call as a legitimate sentence passed by a responsible member of the higher clergy, and one of his Fidaiyan-i Islam assassins carried out the execution in 1945 with the subsequent approval of Khomeini.[3]

During this same period, Khomeini became closely associated with the leading Shiite cleric in Iran, Ayatollah Muhammad Hussein Borujerdi.[4] Though Khomeini carried out a number of important missions for Borujerdi, their policies differed significantly in that Borujerdi opposed the involvement of the ulama in politics, a view completely contrary to that of Khomeini. The relationship gradually cooled to the point that Borujerdi no longer trusted his protégé and distanced himself from him.

But Khomeini continued to use his connection with the senior ayatollah to forward his own political plans, while developing new associations with other higher clerics who shared his own activist views.

Khomeini's political style was always based on shrewd tactical maneuvers and deception, an operational methodology known in Persian as *khodeh* (trickery) and considered a traditional technique of the Shiite leadership.[5] Nevertheless, other ayatollahs, a number ranked higher than Khomeini, did not practice politics in this way. But, as is so often the case, those who can harness their own opportunism to an effective strategy generally gain the advantage in competitive situations. In Khomeini's case, however, the bringing together of an astute political finesse and a violent yet self-righteous ideology in the context of mass alienation from the status quo proved to be a particularly dangerous and untoward combination.

During his exile in the Shiite holy city of Najaf, Khomeini developed through his writings and declarations a powerful political doctrine that captured the imagination of many, including some who were not naturally oriented in terms of Islamic conceptualism. His unremitting castigation of the shah, his insistence that monarchy was incompatible with Islam, and his contention that the regime was involved in an unholy alliance with foreign imperialists struck a responsive chord throughout most of his diversified audience. The controversial aspect of his ideology concerned his views on the repoliticization of Islam, but the implications of this view were understood by only a small perceptive minority of those who listened to his message.

Before the contradictions between the political philosophy of Khomeini and that of many who supported his "crusade" against the shah became evident following the collapse of the regime, the ayatollah had been accepted as the figurehead of the opposition movement. Shaul Bakhash succinctly analyzed the way in which Khomeini accomplished this goal:

> His sensitive antennae carefully attuned to the public temper, he was able to articulate themes and touch on issues that powerfully roused the mass of the people. Islamic fundamentalists and westernized intellectuals, bazaar merchants and the urban masses, came to see in his vision of an Islamic state the chance to realize their very disparate aspirations. Moreover, he had in Iran a network of clerical leaders, religious students, and young political activists devoted to his cause and determined to keep his name at the forefront of the revolutionary agitation.[6]

Millions of Iranians were electrified by Khomeini's constant reference to the political character of Islam.[7] The dominant theme in all his writings is that Muslims have been tricked by oppressive regimes and imperialists into believing that they should remain passive, whereas the religious leaders revered by Islam had dedicated themselves to carrying on a struggle against tyranny and injustice. In a piece condemning the shah's celebration of the Iranian monarchy at Persepolis in 1971, he declared:

> How often have we been told that we must not interfere in the affairs of state! It seems that we have in fact come to believe that it is not our duty to concern ourselves with the affairs of the country and the government, that we have no duty of any kind, and that we should not struggle for justice. In reality, since the very beginning of history, the prophets and scholars of religion have always had the duty of resisting and struggling against monarchs and tyrannical governments. . . .
>
> Come to your senses; awaken Najaf! Let the voice of the oppressed people of Iran be heard throughout the world. . . .
>
> I tell you plainly that a dark, dangerous future lies ahead and that it is your duty to resist and to serve Islam and the Muslim peoples. Protest against the pressure exerted upon our oppressed people every day.[8]

This kind of rhetoric had rarely been articulated by leading clerics in Iran. For most who took issue with the shah's regime it helped legitimize the opposition platform. But for the underprivileged and alienated mass of the people and the disillusioned youth in schools and universities it represented a call to action, a powerful mobilizing force through which they could destroy the structure and orientation of the Pahlevi system. For these it became a multidimensional revolutionary doctrine that could not only overcome the oppressive rule of the shah but also change the whole pattern of class relations, which was at least partly based on the modernist-traditionalist dichotomy. Khomeini had created a vivid imagery of an essential link between Westernization and inequity, between degenerate foreign values and the victimization of the common people in Iran.

Other elements within the broad opposition movement may have shared Khomeini's attitude toward foreign intervention in the country but did not see cultural Westernization as a problem to be addressed. Indeed, many cherished Western political values and sought to employ them in establishing a just and equitable system. Therefore a basic cleavage existed among those arrayed against the shah between the Islamic militants, who supported Khomeini's platform of radical Islamization, and those adhering to a variety of political positions advocating liberalization of the established system. The incompatibility of these differing attitudes became increasingly apparent in the postrevolutionary months and years.

The organized groups that constituted the political spectrum in the early stages of the revolution were oriented in terms of either Islamic resurgence, moderate Islamic reconstruction, or secular reform. Khomeini was the undisputed leader of the militant religious faction. He worked closely with a senior cadre of disciples, the principal members of which were Muhammad Beheshti, Hussein Ali Montazeri, Ali Akbar Hashemi-Rafsanjani, Morteza Motahhari, Abdul Karim Musavi Ardabili, Muhammad Javad Bahonar, and Ali Khamenei. All these men supported Khomeini's concept of an Islamic government in which a *faqih* (jurist) with ultimate authority presided over a political system based entirely on Islamic law and run by a select clerical elite. The primary objective was to achieve a complete Islamization of the society and to remove most vestiges of Western influence and culture in Iran. Since this involved a massive campaign of "purification," it had to be carried out through the strict application of Islamic punishments. Western institutions such as the balance of powers and judicial procedures involving defense council and the right of appeal were regarded as impediments. The political philosophy of liberalism, which was considered a threat to the Islamic aims of the revolution, was also consciously rejected.

A very different religious group under the leadership of Ayatollah Shariatmadari was committed to a moderate reform program based on the concepts of Islamic modernism, originally developed by Muhammad Abduh in Egypt. A number of leading members of the clergy, such as Ayatollah Hasan Qumi-Tabatabai, came to share the positions of this faction, which advocated a combination of liberalism and the revival of Islamic values. They were adamantly opposed to any form of totalitarianism and to a monopolization of power by the clergy.

The liberal parties included the old National front, the moderate left-of-center National Democratic front, and the religious-liberal Iran Freedom movement, with which Mehdi Bazargan was associated. All these organizations favored constitutional democracy and guarantees of personal freedoms. They represented the urban middle and upper middle classes and opposed the shah because of the authoritarian nature of his regime. They were skeptical, however, of radical leftist ideologies and of Islamic resurgence as the basis of the reformed political order. With respect to other elements in the political spectrum, they were closest to the moderate Islamic reform groups, which also respected liberal institutions and values.

The Left in Iran was made up of four major groups. The pro-Soviet Tudeh party, founded in 1941 and the oldest of the leftist organizations, adhered to an orthodox Communist position. Though its influence had declined since the early 1950s, it experienced a brief revival in the early stages of the revolution because of its support for Khomeini. The

Mujahidin-i Khalq-i Iran (Jihadists of the Iranian People), which was formed in the late 1960s by Ahmad Rezai and derived many of its ideas from Ali Shariati and Ayatollah Taleghani, combined a Western-inspired Third World liberationist doctrine with Shiite symbols related to the struggle for justice and legitimacy. The Marxist Fidaiyan-i Khalq (People's Devotees), which had no Islamic content in its platform, emerged at the same time as a separate leftist organization. In the mid-1970s, the Paykar (Struggle) organization was created as a splinter from the Mujahidin-i Khalq but with a secular and Maoist-oriented ideology.

Since all these factions were opposed to the shah, an initial tendency was to emphasize what they had in common and to overlook the sharp ideological differences that separated them. This trend enabled Khomeini to create an image of himself as the titular leader of the anti-Pahlevi revolution and to win the support of groups inherently in conflict with the doctrines he championed. Though many were attracted to his uncompromising rejection of the shah, it was inevitable that a power struggle among the disparate revolutionary camps would ensue after the government had been overthrown.

The shah's regime set in motion the chain of events that led to its own downfall when in January 1978 it arranged for a semiofficial newspaper to publish an article attacking Khomeini. Theological students at Qum staged a mass demonstration following this action, leading to yet another confrontation with the police. These events marked the beginning of the revolution and the assumption by the Islamic activists of a dominant role in the opposition movement.[9] The antishah agitation became increasingly intense over the succeeding months, prompting Khomeini to formulate a strategy for the Islamic militants. His primary aims were to galvanize the drift toward revolution, to avoid any attempt to reach a compromise with the establishment, and to make the foundation of an Islamic government the goal of all the forces of discontent.[10]

Khomeini's leadership became more effective after he moved from Najaf to Paris with the help of Bani-Sadr in October 1978. His improved communication with Teheran allowed him to appoint clerical leaders to serve as his operational deputies and to send declarations by telphone to be transcribed and distributed to hundreds of thousands of receptive readers in Iran.[11] Between his arrival in France and his return to Teheran on February 1, 1979, Khomeini hovered over the mounting unrest like a legendary warrior and a political mastermind with uncanny control over the course of events.

Just prior to departing the country in January 1979, the shah had appointed Shahpur Baktiar of the old National front to take over as prime minister. Baktiar accepted the position only after the shah had agreed to his conditions that freedom of speech and press be restored, political prisoners be released, SAVAK be liquidated, and the Pahlevi fortune be returned to the state.[12] But Khomeini still used the fact of an agreement with the shah to discredit the liberal faction in Iran and to reinforce his position against compromise. Though still in Paris, his remote-control apparatus was so effective that he was able to orchestrate an anti-Baktiar demonstration that involved a million protesters in Teheran, about half that many in Mashhad, and two hundred thousand in Qum.[13] This move not only proved the extent of his power but also established a close working link with the masses that ultimately enabled him to take control of the country.

Khomeini's Consolidation of Power

After his return to Iran, Khomeini began to act as the final authority and to initiate the necessary political maneuvers to ensure the ascendancy of the Islamic resurgence movement and the establishment of an Islamic state. He appointed Bazargan to replace Baktiar, who had lost the backing of the army, as the provisional prime minister. But through his close associates and a lower cadre of religious militants, Khomeini set up a shadow government that was actually more powerful than the official regime. This contradiction in the political structure provided the framework within which the postrevolutionary struggle for power among incompatible factions took place.

The Revolutionary Council, which Khomeini had established in January 1979 as a mixed body to oversee the revolution, changed composition after the formation of the provisional government on February 11. It was now controlled by the new Islamic Republican party (IRP), created by Beheshti and other clerical supporters of Khomeini. This change automatically set up a rivalry between the council, which respected only Islamic credentials and favored an authoritarian religious regime, and Bazargan's provisional government, which emphasized technocratic skills in making political appointments and sought the establishment of a liberal democratic system.[14] The council held the upper hand from the outset, since its own authority was quickly recognized as supreme and because it had a powerful liaison with the masses through its natural affinity with the host of revolutionary committees, guards, and tribunals that had been formed throughout the country.

Khomeini's strategy in dealing with all the parties opposed to his interpretation of Islam and of the revolution was to gradually shift power to the Revolutionary Council and its subordinate organizations, while maintaining control over the alienated masses that regarded him as their deliverer and using an organized system of terror designed to frighten all antagonistic forces into submission. An important step was his creation of the Pasdaran-i Inqilab, or Revolutionary Guards, on May 5, 1979.[15] This paramilitary organization provided the Revolutionary Council and the IRP with military support and also established a degree of control over the unruly revolutionary committees that had sprung up everywhere and were operating independently, although in accordance with Khomeini's own political principles.

The activities of the Revolutionary Guards were complemented on various levels by those of the new secret police, SAVAMA, and of two irregular paramilitary organizations that were used to smash the offices of opposition groups and terrorize all who stood in the way of the Islamic resurgence movement. The Hizbollahis, so named to suggest that they were the "Party of God," were headed by Hadi Ghaffari, and the Mujahidin-i Inqilab-i Islami (Jihadists of the Islamic Revolution) came under the leadership of Behzad Nabavi, both members of Khomeini's senior staff. Recruited from the street and armed mainly with clubs, the rank and file of these terror units was active in breaking up opposition rallies and attacking the headquarters of groups antagonistic to Khomeini.

Khomeini's political strategy, designed to establish an Islamic state and check all attempts to create a liberal democratic system, involved a series of adroit moves to ensure the Islamic alternative. The first of these was in connection with the referendum to determine the new form of government, held at the end of March 1979. Shariatmadari's Islamic People's Republican party (IPRP), the liberal groups, and the leftists wanted to offer the voters a broad range of options, but Khomeini succeeded in restricting the choice to "yes" or "no" on whether it should be an Islamic government. A green slip of paper registered an affirmative vote; a red one indicated a negative response. Michael Fischer suggested that symbolism was intended in this since green is the traditional color of Islam and red was associated with the Ummayad caliph, Yazid. But Bani-Sadr maintained that was not the case inasmuch as red was also the color of Imam Hussein.[16] In any event, the nature of the choice and the voting method produced an overwhelming pro-Islamic majority, an inevitable result given Khomeini's enormous popularity at this stage.

The next order of business was the promulgation of the new constitution.[17] The provisional government presented a working document based largely on liberal concepts and intended to be the starting point of the drafting process for the actual constitution. The views expressed on this document revealed a striking diversity of political opinion, but the basic dispute was over the question of sovereignty. The Islamic militants under Khomeini's leadership wanted real authority to rest with the *faqih* and his advisers, whereas virtually all the other factions believed a legislature representing the people should assume the dominant role. For this reason those in the latter camp favored the convention of a broadly based constituent assembly that would draw up a constitution through democratic procedures. Khomeini tried to avoid this approach by forwarding the idea of an appointed Assembly of Experts to undertake the task. Shariatmadari balked at the proposal, upon which Khomeini suggested a compromise calling for the election of the body. Shariat-madari's agreement proved to be a fatal mistake, since the elections produced an Assembly of Experts with a clerical-IRP majority.

Khomeini enjoined the assembly to work toward a purely Islamic constitution, and Beheshti took charge of the drafting process. The liberal and secular minority in the assembly had virtually no influence over the deliberations, and the final document, which was completed by mid-November 1979, was fashioned after Khomeini's *wilayat-i faqih*. Though the constitution did provide for a popularly elected president and parliament (*majlis*), real power rested with the *faqih* and a Council of Guardians.

The *faqih* was to appoint the six Islamic jurists on the twelve-man Council of Guardians, the chief judiciary officials, the chief-of-staff of the armed forces, most members of the Supreme Defense Council, and the head of the Revolutionary Guards. He also had the right to approve candidates for the presidency and to dismiss an elected president if he had been declared incompetent by the *majlis* or found negligent by the Supreme Court. The Council of Guardians could veto legislation by the *majlis* found to be contrary to Islamic law or the constitution, and the six jurists in this body held final authority on whether or not statutes were legitimate from an Islamic perspective. The Revolutionary Guards became an integral part of the new system and formed the central paramilitary wing of the Islamic order.

Earlier that same November, the U.S. hostage crisis had started, and Bazargan had resigned as prime minister. The open conflict between the Islamic militants and the many other factions that favored basically liberal institutions and procedures had therefore already begun. With the passage of an authoritarian Islamic constitution by the Assembly of Experts, the parties representing moderate religious, secular, centrist, leftist, and ethnic minority ideologies formed an active opposition to Khomeini, who has assumed the role of *faqih*. Shariatmadari's supporters staged a protest in Tabriz in December, but it was effectively checked by the Revolutionary Guards. Shariatmadari himself began to withdraw from the political struggle at this time, in part to avoid factional hostilities and the risk of civil war. This withdrawal undermined the viability of the Islamic modernist camp, and since the secular liberals had also receded, the eclectic doctrine reformers and the Mujahidin-i Khalq remained as Khomeini's main contenders.

Abul Hasan Bani-Sadr now became the central figure in the political controversy. He was popular among the liberals and leftists because of his interpretation of the Islamic revolution in democratic and egalitarian terms and among the masses as a result of his association with Khomeini. Though this relationship with the ayatollah began with Bani-Sadr's admiration of his stalwart opposition to the shah in the 1960s and developed into a close working partnership in the late 1970s, the two men had very different ideologies. Bani-Sadr's idea of good government was not far from the anarchist position, whereas Khomeini advocated an Islamic dictatorship. Bani-Sadr had served on the Assembly of Experts that drafted the constitution and expressed concern that the new system would be absolutist and dominated by bigoted clerics who wanted to force their will on the people. Despite the implicit conflict with the IRP and Khomeini, however, Bani-Sadr was sufficiently well liked throughout the country and respected because of his association with Khomeini to win three-quarters of the votes in the January 1980 presidential election. This victory marked the beginning of a political struggle between Bani-Sadr and the IRP.

Bani-Sadr interpreted the election result as reflecting a widespread popular opposition to the attempts of the clerical class to dominate the new political order. But this reading was really a miscalculation. The alienated segments of the society, which exercised powerful influence through the revolutionary committees all over Iran, were much more receptive to the political position of the IRP than to that of the president. They had voted for Bani-Sadr because they thought he was Khomeini's protégé, and they had not yet perceived the ideological differences between the two men.

The IRP, however, was fully aware of these differences and considered Bani-Sadr's election a setback. Ayatollah Beheshti said that Bani-Sadr represented the same danger of liberalism and that he threatened the revolution as Bazargan had.[18] He regarded liberalism as the greatest enemy of the Islamic resurgence movement because though it was purely a Western and therefore decadent political ideology, many people in Iran were attracted to it. For this reason, he was resolved to oppose Bani-Sadr if he tried to inject liberal principles and institutions into the new order. This difference in perceived roles and commitments set Bani-Sadr and the IRP on a collision course, since the president viewed his own task as one of keeping the Islamic content of the revolution within a liberal framework.

Khomeini and the IRP effectively outmaneuvered Bani-Sadr through two adroit tactical moves. When Khomeini appointed Beheshti as chief justice, the president lost whatever influence he might have had over the judicial system.[19] His political role was further diminished when the

IRP managed to win a majority in the *majlis* by manipulating the electoral system.[20] It had been established that if candidates failed to win an absolute majority, a second round of voting would take place in which a relative majority would be enough to win the seat. Since most of the opposition candidates did not have sufficient public backing to win an absolute majority, this practice meant that in the second round the IRP could win a relative majority for its candidate by forming coalitions with the smaller parties. Other methods to ensure an IRP-dominated *majlis* were the suspension of elections in districts where the opposition parties were more popular and the rejection of elected candidates as "undesirable" if their Islamic credentials were found wanting.

All the opposition factions, of course, objected vehemently to these regulations and practices. But they were unable to alter the situation inasmuch as the Islamic militants who were rapidly seizing power had laid down the laws governing political processes by fiat. As each step in the establishment of the new order was taken, the extent of their absolute control was increased. Their task was made easier by the collaboration of a charismatic and "infallible" titular leader of the revolution and by the support of the masses through revolutionary committees operating without restraint in the absence of very effective central control.

The March elections produced a majority for the IRP and its affiliates, and their domination of the *majlis* was extended by the rejection of some opposition members and the victory of more IRP candidates in the elections for the remaining seats, held shortly thereafter. Bani-Sadr's position was now essentially untenable, given the vulnerability of the presidency embodied in the constitution. A hostile *majlis* working with a *faqih* who shared similar views could easily unseat him. Bani-Sadr could not even choose his own cabinet without the approval of the IRP-controlled parliament. Ultimately, he had to accept Muhammad Ali Rajai as prime minister, despite his own dislike for this man the IRP had forced upon him. Rajai made matters worse for the president by selecting ministers who supported the militant Islamic position.

Bani-Sadr's confrontation with the IRP now became the focal point of the polarized political drama unfolding in Iran. The Islamic militants succeeded in identifying the president with the opposition, thus discrediting him in the eyes of those who venerated Khomeini and approved the Islamization of the governmental system. Bani-Sadr tried to resuscitate his image by concentrating much of his energy on the war with Iraq, which had started in September 1980. But the war actually had the effect of uniting the country behind its Islamic leadership and emphasizing the incompatibilities between Islam as a political order and the secular nationalism advocated by Saddam Hussein and the Baath party. Furthermore, Bani-Sadr's disagreement with the IRP over the handling of the U.S. hostage crisis, and his insistence that professional ability rather than Islamic credentials should be the determining factor in making political appointments, increased his growing unpopularity.

By 1981, the lines were sharply drawn. The opposition, now more clearly identified with the middle and upper middle classes, included various segments of the bourgeoisie, the moderate religious factions, and the parties of the Left. These supported Bani-Sadr in his struggle against the IRP. An important link was established between the president and the Mujahidin-i Khalq. The Islamic militants, supported by the lower middle and lower classes, were led by the IRP and affiliated parties and sympathetic independents. This side had the advantages of mass backing, control of the political processes, and the blessing of Khomeini. It also had an effective paramilitary wing in the form of the Revolutionary Guards, the Hizbollahis, and other irregular units, as well as a close affinity with the revolutionary committees throughout the country.

During the first half of 1981, the IRP mounted a campaign against Bani-Sadr, appealing to the public, utilizing the media, and employing occasional violence through its paramilitary facilities. Their task was also made easier by the developing pattern of arrests, convictions by revolutionary tribunals, executions, and floggings. The climate of terror helped to undermine the opposition, which was already weakened by its lack of cohesiveness. Khomeini's role in these events was somewhat equivocal.[21] He continued to hold Bani-Sadr in some esteem because of the younger man's support and cooperation before the revolution. He therefore made several attempts to achieve a reconciliation between the president and the IRP. But Bani-Sadr's undisguised opposition to the governmental system and to leading figures in the IRP finally turned Khomeini against him. In a last effort in June to avoid the untoward repercussions of an impeachment, he called on the president to repent. This appeal was of no avail, and the ayatollah came to the conclusion that Bani-Sadr was in some way associated with a broad secular movement to dismantle the Islamic political institutions of the country.

At this point, the IRP sought to impeach the president. After a debate on June 20–21, the *majlis* voted overwhelmingly to declare him incompetent, as throngs in the streets shouted their approval. In late July, Bani-Sadr and the Mujahidin-i Khalq leader, Masud Rajavi, fled on a commandeered aircraft to Paris. There they formed the National Council of Resistance (NCR), an organization based on a pact concluded earlier by the two men and dedicated to the overthrow of Khomeini's regime and its replacement by a democratic system.

Opposition groups moved without delay to launch an armed campaign against the IRP.[22] On June 28, 1981, a bomb exploded at the party's headquarters, killing seventy-two of the leaders, including Ayatollah Beheshti. This attack was attributed to the Mujahidin-i Khalq but was never claimed by that group and remains a mystery. Another bomb attack at the prime minister's office on August 30 took the lives of Rajai, who had become president, Bahonar, the new prime minister, and police chief Vahid Dastgerdi. A week later, the prosecutor-general was assassinated. Ultimately, however, the government prevailed over the opposition in this violent confrontation, conducting raids against the Mujahidin in particular and carrying out regular public executions lasting through 1982, after which they became less frequent.

The Islamic Government: Theory and Practice

Khomeini's theory of Islam is that it is primarily a sociopolitical order derived entirely from divine sources and not in any respect the product of cultural exchange. The accompanying theory of Islamic government is based on the premise that it is possible to replace the degenerate remnants of Islam found throughout the contemporary Muslim world with a genuine Islamic order. If such a system is properly constructed and administered, it will be just and perfect in every sense because it is founded on the *sharia*, run by the clergy, and devoid of contaminating attributes and influences. These theories show why Western traditions subsumed under the heading of "democracy" have no place whatsoever in his conceptual framework. Furthermore, virtually any means deemed efficacious may be employed to ensure the successful establishment of the Islamic ruling institution as he conceived it.

This theoretical construct, which reflects the major themes of most present-day Islamic neofundamentalism, contains three demonstrable flaws, which became evident when it was put into practice in Iran. First, the presentation of Islam as principally a political doctrine effectively obscures the spiritual and humanistic attributes of the religion. Yet in reality these nonpolitical dimensions are ultimately more important. Second, the idea of imposing and maintaining an ostensibly pristine sociopolitical order by authoritarian means does not take into consideration the universal frailties of human nature. In particular, it is axiomatically incapable of dealing with the problem of power, the perennial tendency of those who have it to abuse it if they are not prevented by institutionalized restrictions. Third, the rejection of Islamic civilization's eclectic origins is not only historically inaccurate but precludes the utilization of Western political traditions that could have provided safeguards against monopolization of power and violations of human rights.

The problems inherent in this theoretical formulation inevitably produced a highly repressive political system when an Islamic government headed by Khomeini was established in Iran. The shrewd tactical methods through which the militant neofundamentalists outmaneuvered their opponents were only the beginning of a reign of terror designed to obliterate all manifestations of opposition and keep the population passive and obedient.

Following the dismissal of Bani-Sadr as president in June 1981 and the subsequent attacks on IRP leaders, the regime launched a systematic roundup of all people, regardless of age or sex, who could in any way be considered enemies of the Islamic order. The major targets were the active leftist organizations, especially the Mujahidin-i Khalq-i Iran, and people of the Bahai faith, thought to be subversives. The victims were apprehended, imprisoned, tortured, and frequently executed after summary trials without rights of defense or appeal. The most intense period of such activity was during the months following the incidents of June 1981, but it has continued as standard practice up to the present.

There is some uncertainty as to how many people were executed between Bani-Sadr's departure from office on June 20, 1981, and the end of the year. Amnesty International, which cites only proven cases and describes its own figures as "minimal," verified 2,444 executions of this type during the period.[23] The well-informed Iranian journalist, Amir Taheri, claims that 6,000 persons paid the death penalty in the course of the same six months.[24] Amnesty International's figures of confirmed political executions in Iran are 624 for 1982, 399 for 1983, 661 for 1984, and 470 for 1985, but the total from the beginning of the revolution in early 1979 and the end of 1985 is 6,578.[25] A conservative estimate of the actual number would be twice that number.

Included among those executed have been children of both sexes between ten and fifteen years of age accused of supporting the Mujahidin.[26] Citing Khomeini as his theological authority, Muhammad Muhammadi-Gilani, one of three prosecutors presiding over the execution process, announced that the death sentence could be passed against children: "A nine-year-old girl is considered an adult in Islam. So such a girl is responsible for her acts and can be executed if she tries to war on Allah."[27] Assadollah Lajevardi, another of the prosecutors, reportedly said: "Even if a twelve-year-old is found participating in an armed demonstration, he will be shot. The age doesn't matter."[28]

Aside from the indifference to the age of those executed and the frequent executions of people who had never been charged or tried, the use of torture, either to extract information about political activities, the names and addresses of other political activists, and the location of safehouses, or to induce prisoners to appear on television to repent their political beliefs or actions, became a standard and widespread practice in 1981 and continues to the present.[29] Sometimes people have been tortured for no reason at all except to inflict pain as a form of punishment. One prisoner testified that at Gofar Dasht Prison, "there wasn't a moment you couldn't hear the shouts of people being subjected to torture." The most notorious place of detention is Evin Prison in Teheran, built by the former shah.

The most common form of torture has been flogging, sometimes with heavy cables that rip the flesh, sometimes on the soles of the feet. Other practices include suspension from the ceiling for prolonged periods, electric shocks, holding the head under water, and burning with cigarettes and electric irons. Prisoners are often pushed from one guard to another while being beaten, kicked, and punched. They are routinely deprived of food and water for the first forty-eight hours of incarceration. They are tortured at times when food has been digested to avoid vomiting. They are subjected to various kinds of psychological torture, including being forced to load the sometimes maimed bodies of executed former cell mates and relatives onto trucks. They are also victimized by various forms of sexual abuse, mainly rape and sodomy.

Punishments for alleged moral crimes, such as adultery, alcohol consumption, and theft, include stoning to death, flogging, and amputation, a new machine having been installed for the last purpose. Though these may be specified in Islamic law, they are nevertheless simply forms of torture. Furthermore, their employment is mainly an aspect of the general campaign of terror used by the regime to maintain control of the country.

This system of repression is neither accidental nor unorganized. It is a basic part of the Islamic regime's attempt to consolidate its power and force a particular lifestyle on the population. Incarceration, torture, and executions are carried out by the Pasdaran and local revolutionary committees, which are the principal agencies through which the government keeps all segments of the populace under its supervision. Khomeini is fully aware of the procedures employed. He considers them a "necessary surgery" to purify Iran and calls on his followers, especially children, to watch the activities of everyone around them so that they may become spies of Allah.[30] The country was thus brought under authoritarian rule imposed by violence and maintained by degradation and terror.

The same kind of repression that existed under the shah's regime was continued after the revolution, only on a larger scale.[31] In this light, Ayatollah Borujerdi's alleged warning about Khomeini seems like an accurate prophesy. Discussing the question of his successor with loyal friends, he is said to have commented: "Follow anyone you like, anyone except Khomeini. For following Khomeini shall lead you knee-deep in blood."[32]

Another aspect of Khomeini's theoretical formulation concerns the relationship between the Islamic government in Iran and the external world. His concept of himself as a forerunner of the "hidden Imam" implied a global mission. He therefore considered it obligatory for the regime to carry on a new crusade: "We should try to export our revolution to the world. We should set aside the thought that we do not export our revolution. . . . If we remain in an enclosed environment we shall definitely face defeat."[33] This externalization of Khomeini's movement is, however, based on more than idealistic principle or its leader's egotistical self-image. It is required to sustain the momentum of the revolution and to protect Iran's advantages in its regional setting.

An initial decline in the popularity of the revolution had been temporarily arrested by the U.S. hostage crisis, but popular support for the regime was more effectively maintained by the Iraqi attack in September 1980 and the prolonged war that followed. Khomeini described this new development as "a blessing from Allah" and concentrated much of his attention on maintaining a close communication link with the thousands of young people who had expressed their willingness to die for his cause and had thus been diverted from any inclination they may have had to identify with the leftist opposition.[34]

The Iran-Iraq war has gone on unabated for years. The major reason for this has been Khomeini's complete unwillingness to agree to compromises that could make peace possible. Indeed, he has adamantly insisted that the war be pursued until Iraq is defeated and Saddam Hussein's regime removed. He reinforced this position in a speech on February 10, 1987, in which he decribed Iran's struggle as a holy crusade and said the Islamic government would "make war until victory."[35] This kind of statement is effective in preserving the ideological commitment of large segments of the youth to the regime and the war. It also keeps the war itself going, thus serving another of Khomeini's aims.

Iran's regional status is derived largely from its dominant position in the Gulf.[36] Its principal challenger in this region is Iraq, which has formidable natural and human resources and which assumed in the late 1970s a role as protector of the Arab states in the Gulf. To preserve Iran's regional ascendancy, it is therefore necessary to curtail Iraqi power and keep the other Arab Gulf states on the defensive.

A deliberate campaign to achieve these ends was initiated in September 1979, when Iran revived its claim to Bahrain and declared its intention to promote Islamic neofundamentalist agitation throughout the Gulf area.[37] This provocation became more intense and led Saddam Hussein to launch an attack on Iran a year later. This move was partly because of his protective posture toward the Arab states in the Gulf and partly because he found the Iranian regime increasingly unfriendly yet vulnerable as a result of the political divisiveness within the country. The war did not prevent Iran from carrying on its subversive activities in the region, however, and at the end of 1981 the government attempted unsuccessfully to initiate a revolt in Bahrain.

Though a definitive victory against Iraq seems unlikely, Saddam Hussein's power has been greatly diminished and the neighboring Arab states remain in a defensive position with regard to Iran. All these countries are also sensitive to the existence of sizable Shiite communities within their own borders. They form a majority in Iraq and Bahrain and a significant segment of the work force in the oil fields. In terms of the strategic balance, therefore, the war has to a limited extent achieved the goals of the Iranian regime.

The cost of the war is another matter. The Iranian casualties have certainly exceeded half a million, a number confirmed by a U.S. Senate staff report in August 1984 and by a reliable scholar, Adeed Dawisha, in November 1986.[38] Many of those killed and wounded have been extremely young members of the Pasdaran and Baseej (Mobilization Force) volunteers whose dedication to Khomeini and the regime has led them to serve as "human waves," sacrificing themselves as they pave the way for the advance of the regular army.[39] The willingness of Khomeini and other leaders of the Islamic Republic to accept this kind of unnecessary slaughter of Iranian youth raises serious questions as to their interpretation of Islam and its role in the contemporary era.

Khomeini's view of Islam locked in a cosmic struggle with a hostile external world led not only to the war with Iraq but to the isolation of Iran in its regional environment. His conception of Islamic resurgence as a transnational movement and his antipathy toward monarchy and secular nationalism established the ideological basis of a conflict situation between the Teheran regime and many other Middle Eastern countries. In referring to the missionary role of the new government, the Iranian constitution implied the inauguration of an Islamic crusade directed initially against neighboring states considered only nominally Muslim by neofundamentalist standards.

Egypt, Turkey, Pakistan, Morocco, Saudi Arabia, the Gulf sheikhdoms, and Jordan all had friendly relations with the United States, which Khomeini regarded as the "Great Satan" and the enemy of Islam. Iraq, Turkey, and Egypt were run by secular regimes espousing doctrines of nationalism that were anathema to the Islamic resurgence movement. Egypt had made peace with Israel, another cardinal sin. Saudi Arabia, the Gulf states, Morocco, and Jordan were under monarchical rule, which Khomeini had declared to be contrary to the political principles of Islam. All these countries perceived Khomeini as a threat, and the government in Iran considered them as potential adversaries and as targets in its mission to export the revolution.

Iraq, however, was the immediate archenemy, not only because it stood as the principal barrier to Iran's regional supremacy but also because it symbolized everything Khomeini was against. It had made a deal with the shah over the Kurdish issue and the Shatt al-Arab dispute in 1975. Its leadership was largely Sunni, though more than half the population was Shiite. It was committed to the pronounced secularism and Arab nationalism of the Baath party, and in this sense its ideology was at the opposite pole from Islamic neofundamentalism. It had developed a close relationship with Saudi Arabia and Jordan in particular and was on good terms with a number of other Arab states, which gave it moral and material support. It was actively trying to prevent the exportation of Iranian neofundamentalism into the Gulf sheikhdoms and to popularize the concept of an innate Arab-Iranian rivalry dating back to the Arab conquest of Iran in the seventh century.

The Khomeini regime has not been successful, however, in its endeavors to enlist Arab support for its brand of Islamic revolution, with the exception of some headway it has made among the Lebanese Shiites. This failure results partly because a sense of ethnic national identity is still widespread in most Arab countries. Even the Shiites of Iraq have for the most part remained loyal to Saddam Hussein in the Iran-Iraq war. But the major reason has been that, in Adeed Dawisha's words,

> it had become clear to many Arabs that Iran's revolution had stalled. The news of atrocities and cruelties aimed at its own people in Iran painted a reality that did not correspond to the ayatollahs' sterling claims. The Moslem Arab could now see that in Islamic Iran, neither harmony nor humanity reigned. So as the revolution turned on its own children, those on the other side of the Gulf began to turn away from it.[40]

The provocative demonstration by Iranian Shiites in Mecca on July 31, 1987, resulting in hundreds of casualties, intensified the alienation of most Arab Sunnis from the Teheran regime.

The distinct Shiite character of the Iranian regime may be a factor in the predominantly Sunni Arab attitude toward Khomeini and the revolution. But the more important reality is that when Islamic neofundamentalism was actually put into practice, the problems of perception and judgment inherent in its own visionary outlook inevitably came to the surface. This involved not only cruelty in suppressing opposition and sending children to die on the battlefield but also corruption and power rivalries in the political sphere.

Ayatollah Khalkhali, one of Khomeini's favorites and at one time a merciless magistrate in the revolutionary courts presiding over the purge, was eventually accused of accepting $25 million in bribes and was dismissed as antinarcotics judge when he was unable to provide an adequate defense.[41] Another Khomeini protégé, Hojjat al-Islam Maadikhah, was removed as minister of Islamic orientation because of a rumored scandal involving him and a former television news broadcaster. An even more sensitive development at the heart of the Islamic religious establishment in Iran was the dismissal in 1983 of nearly one-third of the principal prayer leaders throughout the country for what was described as "loose conduct,"[42] presumably corruption.

The decline in the moral character of the Islamic regime is also reflected in the struggle for power among the *mullahs*. Exasperated by the political machinations of the clerical class, Khomeini said to them in a speech to the Assembly of Experts: "You cannot fool me by saying that your quarrels are about the interests of Islam. You are fighting for power and I know it."[43] More recently, the question of the succession to Khomeini has become a key issue in the high-level rivalry between Ayatollah Hussein Ali Montazeri, designated as Khomeini's successor over two years ago, and Hojjat al-Islam Ali Akbar Hashemi-Rafsanjani, the speaker of the *majlis*.[44] Montazeri has been identified with the purist approach to neofundamentalist ideological positions, and Hashemi-Rafsanjani is regarded as more pragmatic and open to compromise, especially in international relations. Yet the competition between the two men is more a conflict of personalities and a power game than a question of divergent views. Most important, it has little to do with a reevaluation of the revolution itself. Yet without a genuine attempt to take stock of what has been going on since 1979, the deterioration of the political situation will certainly continue, while the rest of the Middle East and the Muslim world consider other approaches to the revival of Islam in the twentieth century.

7

Islam and the Future

Interpretive Issues

The attempt to sort out the character and implications of the various political experiments tried in the post-Ottoman Middle East raises substantive questions regarding the validity of different interpretive approaches. Any analysis of the doctrines seeking the establishment of a secular nationalist order or an Islamic reform program or an Islamic state necessarily involves some position on the ideal model of secular nationalism or the attributes of genuine Islam. Theories differ on the true nature of each as a sociopolitical system and on the endeavors to use them as guidelines in the task of reconstruction. Some are polemical and opinionated; others are scholarly and profound, with a variety of shades between the two extremes. An effort will be made here to formulate an analytical framework that combines a comparative evaluation of conflicting interpretations with a realistic consideration of the actual circumstances prevailing in Middle Eastern society at the end of the twentieth century.

Secularization and nationalism, and the concomitant subordination of Islam as a guiding sociopolitical principle, became the dominant themes in the public life of much of the Middle East after World War I. As interrelated doctrines in the popularized nationalist ideologies designed to mobilize and reshape many of the countries in the area, they created new behaviorial models and loyalties. Certainly they represented a sharp break with the past and generated new hopes and aspirations. In time, however, their use as platforms for ambitious development programs proved disappointing. The political malpractices and monopolization of power by the regimes that upheld them as a preferred alternative to Islam made them disenchanting as well.

The shortcomings of the nationalist experiment, which have been investigated in this book, led to a climate of reevaluation and stock-taking, sometimes revolutionary in orientation, that has had a profound impact on the entire area. But as yet almost no attempt has been made to find out exactly why secular nationalism has lost some of its appeal and in certain cases become more disruptive than creative and beneficial. A major reason, discussed earlier in this book, is that the kind of nationalism that took root in the Middle East was a limited reproduction of the Western original. Though committed to liberation from foreign control and fostering a sense of responsibility to common aspirations, its political philosophy provided no safeguards against the misuse of power.

The most durable forms of nationalism in the West were related to broader movements seeking liberalization, carefully defined limits of authority, and protection of the rights of citizens. Though imperfect in many instances, this liberal nationalism at least had the theoretical basis that guaranteed the continuity and progressive revision of itself as a viable institution. John Pocock has developed a convincing interpretation of the American revolutionary movement as the culmination of English opposition thought and Renaissance political theory.[1] His analysis of the contribution made by the founders of the United States to the concept of just and mature government reveals an intellectual depth, drawn from European sources and later perfected in the New World, that became an inseparable part of contemporary Western democracy.

The absence of such a tradition in the formulation of nationalism in the Middle East suggests a direct relationship between a weakly developed political doctrine and governmental systems that have difficulty integrating their constituents in an open and equitable system. The problem with nationalism in the Middle East may not be the institution itself but the superficial way it was formulated from only partially understood Western models. There is also the argument that the peoples of the area were not ready for European-style liberal nationalism because of limited educational resources and an incompatible sociopolitical orientation. Although this may be an aspect of the problem, the capacity of Middle Easterners to change their attitudes and outlook radically in a short space of time has been demonstrated in some cases, notably in Turkey. Misinterpretation of borrowed concepts was therefore a more important factor in the limitations of nationalism in this area.

Developing a reliable assessment of the Islamic tradition and an evaluation of the divergent contemporary approaches to it is a difficult task. The position taken in this book and accepted by most scholars is that Islam evolved from a religious doctrine into a multifaceted civilization representing a composite of diverse cultural elements brought within an Islamic framework. Islam has also grown with time, expanding its perspectives and elaborating its world view. It has never been static or rigid but rather a legacy that accrued a variety of often highly refined and profound attributes over the centuries. Because of this and its own understanding of man's relationship to God, Islam is historically oriented and attaches great importance to what transpires among people in time. Though Islam acquired a political dimension as a result of this concern, it has had considerable difficulty with problems of power and order. Its humanistic aspects therefore became more durable and ultimately more fulfilling parts of the heritage.

Another observation about Islam, one almost universally accepted, is that in recent centuries it has been relatively stagnant and uncreative intellectually, as well as corrupt and degenerate in the sociopolitical sphere. This was a major reason for the decline of the Ottoman Empire and other political entities in the Middle East and the subsequent intrusion of the great powers into the area. It was also the cause of the diversified search for reform and reconstruction that has been the subject of this book.

The state of siege that beset Islam in the Middle East during the nineteenth and twentieth centuries led to a debate among Muslims as to what should be done to remedy the situation. There were different opinions among those who did not opt for the secular Westernizing solution. The conservative *ulama*, undoubtedly still the largest single grouping within the clergy, continued in their traditional nonpolitical role preaching a rather uninspiring version of Islam and protecting their interests by avoiding any conflict with the ruling elite. Mohammed Arkoun, admittedly partisan on the subject, has described the limitations of these conservatives in vivid terms:

> Intellectually and culturally, the official Islam of the *ulama* in the era which concerns us was marked by an extreme doctrinal poverty. For a long time Islamic thinking had allowed itself to fall into the dogmatic repetition of several handbooks of law, grammar, exegesis and history. . . . Cut off from classical sources as well as from the spiritual influence of the great sufi masters, popular Islam was in its turn victim of the debasement of the social imagination and of the collective sensitivity.[2]

During the latter part of the nineteenth century, there was a sharp break with this inept form of Islam by the Islamic modernists. The interpretive issue in the controversy surrounding Muhammad Abduh and the *salafiyya* thinkers is whether their endeavors represent a revival of genuine Islam or a subtle manipulation of concepts designed to make Western institutions and values acceptable by presenting them as Islamic in origin. Daniel Pipes took the position that the modernists were trying to reconcile Islamic law with Western culture. Nevertheless, he insisted, "Equating Islam with the ideals of liberalism obviously requires a radical reinterpretation of the faith."[3] He also argued that the modernists emphasized the Quran over such other sources of Islam as the *hadith* (traditions of the Prophet), consensus, and analogy, because the Quran is less precise and therefore more adaptable. Their contention was that "Each generation must reread the Qur'an, reach its own consensus, and use its logical facilities to change the law and make it current." Pipes rejected this approach as a way of subordinating Islam to the requirements of change: "The Qur'an in their hands becomes a collection of disjointed quotes and proof texts. Instead of endeavoring to comprehend God's will, they use it to confirm preconceived notions." He concluded that Islamic modernism "is a tired movement, locked in place by the unsoundness of its premises and arguments."[4]

Inasmuch as Pipes also took issue with the neofundamentalists, the thrust of his book is that since modernization requires Westernization, the only real choice open to contemporary Muslims is emulation of the West.[5] This summary relegation of Islam to the category of obsolescence overlooks not only the continuity of a living tradition but also the problems that have attended the Westernization process in the Middle East. Marshall Hodgson asserted: "The [Islamic] heritage does remain as an active cultural force, even as a single whole."[6] At the same time, he recognized that the impact of the West in modern times "ushered in a new period in the world's history, in which the bulk of mankind . . . came to form a global society of closely interacting nations." But this world scope did not pose a problem for Muslims because Islam "had not been isolated even in its origins, since it presupposed the wider historical complex of which the Occident formed a part."[7]

For Hodgson, the challenge confronting contemporary Islam in the Middle East and elsewhere was to find a way of preserving its own heritage in the context of the universal cosmopolitanism that grew out of the encounter between the West and the rest of the world in our own times. Unlike Pipes, therefore, he had a positive attitude toward Muhammad Abduh and the Islamic modernists, whose approach represents the only realistic and satisfactory solution to the problem.

In Hodgson's view, Muhammad Abduh did not reject the Islamic tradition as it existed in the nineteenth century in favor of Westernization but to revive *ijtihad*, "the free exploration within the originally established rules of legal inquiry and the moral norms of Islam, of what was best here and now."[8] Although admitting that Abduh was influenced by modern European thinkers, he noted that the Egyptian reformer was particularly drawn to the ideas of Auguste Comte, who championed science and positivism but affirmed man's need for religion. Abduh felt that Islam was naturally disposed to such a combination of science and religion and devoted much of his life to reviving and blending these compatible dimensions of the Muslim-Arab heritage. If this approach involved a marriage between Islam and certain aspects of modern Western culture, the same result can be expressed in a different way. As Hodgson put it, Abduh's "influence was in part a personally moral one: he fought all superstition and corruption in the name of self-reliant honesty and efficiency . . . he was bent on showing to modernly trained men the validity and relevance of Islam as a faith."[9]

The theory of Islamic modernism was never fully developed or considered for any kind of implementation. Eventually the whole idea of Islamic reform was radically altered to the point that it bore little resemblance to what Muhammad Abduh had in mind. Yet the new neofundamentalist concept of reform became a more controversial issue because of the activist role it came to assume in Middle East politics.

The neofundamentalists seek to obliterate all traces of modernity from Middle Eastern political life and to restore what they see as the original Islam, literally interpreted and forcibly imposed. They have little or no reference to the legacy of Islam as a civilization developed over centuries. As the French scholar, Gilles Kepel, phrased it, "What distinguishes the extremist Islamicist movement from the bulk of Muslims as far as the golden age is concerned is that the former blot out history in favour of the reactivation of the founding myth, while the latter accommodate themselves to the history of Muslim societies."[10]

In failing to grasp the content and significance of the medieval Islamic synthesis, the resurgence ideologues developed a unidimensional concept of Islam based principally on its political and legal precepts. Their dogmas were often highly generalized, even simplistic and anti-intellectual, because their primary practical aim was to arouse the masses through emotive metaphors expressed in common colloquial language. They also played on the grievance psychology engendered by the failures and malpractices of the nationalist order.

The inherent problems in the neofundamentalist doctrine and program have been analyzed from a number of perspectives. The comments of two scholars seem particularly apt. Daniel Pipes, whose interpretation of Islamic modernism may seem based on hasty conclusions, made some thoughtful observations about the significance of the position of the neofundamentalists.[11] Maintaining that they have, in effect, converted the *sharia* into an ideology, he pointed out that the result is "a vague 'Islamic order,' unrestrained by objective standards, [which] becomes whatever fundamentalists wish it to be." This ambiguity creates a fluid and unpredictable situation in which those who have power, whether in an organization or an Islamic state, can impose their interpretation of Islam on others, even if it is patently heretical. Another problem is that "when fundamentalists codify the Shari'a, they petrify an evolving rule and make it restrictive. The law had always adapted to time and place in small but key ways, but fundamentalists make it a fixed doctrine, leaving no room for individual responses." In the end, Pipes believed, the Islam of the neofundamentalists "begins to usurp the role of God."

Since the Islamic resurgence movement actively sought the overthrow of existing regimes deemed corrupt and contaminated, it was axiomatically revolutionary. Yet though Shiism is receptive to the idea of revolt, there is distinct resistance to it in Sunni theory. For this reason Sayyid Qutb and other neofundamentalist ideologues revived the political philosophy of Ibn Taymiyya (1268–1328) in an attempt to legitimize revolution from a Sunni point of view. More specifically, Qutb was trying to use Ibn Taymiyya to justify his doctrine of insurrection against *jahili* regimes, derived largely from the Pakistani theologian, Sayyid Abul Ala Mawdudi.[12] Nevertheless, as Emmanuel Sivan has correctly observed with regard to Ibn Taymiyya:

> A firebrand he surely was, but hardly a revolutionary. . . . His whole endeavor was to cleanse Islam of the dross accumulated during centuries of decline . . . and not even hostile sultans and emirs accused him of sedition. . . . Never did Ibn Taymiyya challenge the legitimacy of any particular sultan. . . . He was indicted as a . . . 'deviant' from theological norms, but never as a harbinger of insurgency.[13]

Despite the liberties taken by Sayyid Qutb in creating a new image of the late medieval thinker, "The Ibn Taymiyya message, as reinterpreted by Sayyid Qutb, . . . continued to transmit in cultural code the frustrations and animosities vis-à-vis modernity, and to legitimize in Sunni terms the deeply felt protest against the [Egyptian] regime, which upholds its values."[14] Qutb and his mentor, Mawdudi, thus converted Islamic neofundamentalism into a challenging opposition to the status quo, equating modernity with *jahiliyya,* calling for a remedy through rebellion, and prescribing a solution to the problem of making the resurgence movement a countersociety and a vanguard of radical re-Islamization.[15] Khomeini, who was influenced by Qutb and Mawdudi, accomplished a similar and more successful result in Iran. What remains very questionable, however, is whether the militant movement that these personalities helped galvanize draws on the entirety of the Islamic tradition or a limited segment.

All these interpretive issues must be carefully weighed as we probe for answers to the Islamic question in Middle East politics. In final analysis, however, each investigator has to develop a particular theory, based on the individual's own appraisal of the circumstances, motivations, value systems, and sociocultural dynamics that determine commitment and behavior. All these considerations should relate, however, to an analysis of actual needs and the limitations and possibilities that exist with regard to their fulfillment.

Islam and the West in
Middle East Political Thought

Secular nationalism and Islamic resurgence represent diametrically opposed approaches to the sociopolitical reconstruction of the Middle East. Their encounter over the years as competing ideologies has been openly hostile and often bitter. One of the paradoxes of contemporary politics in the area, however, is that both the secularists and the Islamic revolutionaries have derived their doctrinal systems from Islamic and Western sources. The irreversible combination of these two traditions is reflected in this incongruous phenomenon.

The Islamic components in each political creed include the utopianism of the early Muslim world view, the unresolved issues of power and authority, and a pattern of interaction involving myth and resignation. The visionary picture of the ideal *umma* was inspired by the model of Muhammad's rule in Medina. It was based on the concept of a dedicated and united community seeking to fulfill its historic mission under the direction of a pious and enlightened caliph. The patent idealism of this image understandably encountered difficulties in the real world of history. In the medieval period, the problem was resolved by adjustments in the conceptual framework and practical measures taken by the *ulama*. Most contemporary neofundamentalists, however, take the premises of the myth at face value, leaving them far less capable of dealing with the contradictions between theory and reality.

Dedication and unity were often thwarted by circumstances, but this deficiency was concealed by a leadership tradition that preserved executive power for centuries. Though frequently of questionable legitimacy, Islamic government survived from one age to the next because there was a general consensus that a facade of harmony and unity was more important than equity and the right of opposition.

In the modern context, this concentration of authority in an exalted leader is evident in both secular and Islamic neofundamentalist political structures. The only difference is that charisma has become more important because the citizenship concept made mass appeal necessary. Mustafa Kemal Atatürk and Gamal Abdul Nasser became the prototypes of the populist national hero, leading their people out of a despotic and superstitious past into a new and just age filled with hope and opportunity. Khomeini exercised a similar kind of charismatic appeal, galvanizing the antishah movement with his uncompromising condemnation of the regime and projecting an image of himself as a "deliverer." In all these cases, there were opposition elements, but these were either suppressed by force and cunning or prevented from assuming an effective role by the popularity of the leader and his platform.

The leadership syndrome, which pervades much of the Middle East, is really a recapitulation of the political tradition that developed in Islam during its earlier centuries. This syndrome in turn engendered issues of power and authority, partly resolved in the formative period but perpetuated with most of the component problems in the contemporary era. With a harnessed judiciary and the absence of a representative legislative function, the political supremacy of premodern Islamic rulers was relatively unchecked, though some administrative autonomy existed in a number of cases. Sovereignty resided with the wielder of power, and this power was hardly ever challenged for the sake of preserving the stability and cohesion of whatever Muslim community was involved.

Contemporary Middle East governments, with a few exceptions, operate in the same fashion but with greater control over their constituencies. Many of the secular nationalist regimes have monopolized power and wealth to an incredible extent and deal repressively with all forms of opposition. Most of the Islamic resurgence organizations are also authoritarian and regimented, while the Islamic government in Iran is absolutist in forcing conformity to its program. Unapologetic about its disinterest in democratic practices, it insists that only an Islamic dictatorship can exterminate Western culture and revive the sociopolitical principles of Islam.

Related to this kind of political orientation is a pattern of behavior in which myth and resignation are prominent ingredients. Here again, the contemporary manifestation is a partial recapitulation of the Islamic past. In former centuries, the ruling institution generally enlisted the support of the religious establishment to reinforce its legitimacy while leaving the *ulama* free to preside over many administrative functions. Since there was no way the society could challenge this kind of status quo, the constituents accommodated themselves to it. In modern times, the ruling elites employ more deceptive methods to preserve their power. Most regimes in the area engage in an elaborate myth-making process designed to gloss over various forms of malpractice and repression or the inability to keep promises and achieve designated goals.

The secular nationalist ideologies are based on generalized and often romantic aspirations, and those who forward them are pictured as virtually faultless heroes of the national cause. Neofundamentalist doctrines are equally sweeping in what they claim to represent, and the organizations that propagate them pose as the vanguard of a divinely ordained historical event of ultimate importance. In both cases, the cult of the personality forms an integral part of the myth's mystique. Leaders such as Atatürk, Nasser, Asad, Saddam Hussein, and Ayatollah Khomeini are portrayed everywhere on posters and lapel buttons. This publicity is designed to give the leader the appearance of being superhuman, a way of exalting the ideology he champions and covering up any weaknesses or contradictions in its position. The general public, often overawed by such histrionics, as well as terrified by the brutal suppression of opposition, has to acquiesce unless some viable avenue of revolt opens for it.

Those aspects of Middle East political thought derived from Islam, whether in secular or neofundamentalist ideology, represent the very dimensions of the religion most problematical historically. Discarding the determinist theory that societies are locked in a repetition syndrome from which they cannot escape, it is possible to look at this situation as subject to change. If, as has been suggested frequently in this book, the humanist traditions of Islam could be revived, some of the political problems carried over from the past could at least be ameliorated, if not removed. Without such a development, however, the despotism passed down through the centuries and identified as a source of decline when the idea of reform was first introduced will almost certainly continue indefinitely in different forms. Nevertheless, as this continuance would mean a lack of progress or regression, the mood of the people seems not to be receptive to that kind of stagnation.

There are also Western components in both the secular and neofundamentalist ideologies of the Middle East. The Western origin of the secular nationalist doctrines is fairly obvious except for the often overlooked fact that the borrowed concept was transposed to the Middle East with some defects in the development of political principles. This raises some question as to how "Western" the various Middle Eastern nationalisms really are. Though secular and utilitarian in orientation, their lack of safeguards against the monopolization of power links them more to Islamic than to European political tradition.

The Islamic resurgence leaders and organizations consciously spurned most aspects of Western culture. They were, nevertheless, influenced by certain modes of European political behavior. Daniel Pipes maintained: "Ironically, in an effort to stave off Western ideologies, fundamentalists radically change their religion and direct it along Western lines."[16] Acting on the citizenship concept, itself Western in origin, the neofundamentalists inadvertently imitated European models in their revolutionary style and their methods of galvanizing the commonality through populist activism. They may also have taken something from examples of demagogic leadership and mass manipulation found in some forms of European political practice, such as fascism and communism.

Daniel Pipes summed up this paradoxical aspect of militant Islamic neofundamentalism succinctly by observing that "self-conscious rejection of the West changes a Muslim as much as adopting its ways. Maududi and Khomeini are thoroughly modern men."[17] In the final analysis, then, while the Islamic modernists were trying to use the best of the Western legacy in an Islamic context, the neofundamentalists were unconsciously borrowing the more questionable aspects of that same tradition in their quest for power and influence. The differences between the two approaches to Islamic reform are therefore considerable.

The existence of Islamic and Western conceptualism in both kinds of contemporary ideology points to the inescapable reality that Middle Eastern sociopolitical orientation is the product of a cultural composite. If such a combination is inevitable, then the major task of the future is to find ways of making the most constructive and valid components of each tradition compatible parts of a modern synthesis. This was done in the past, and there is no reason it cannot be done in the present.

The Quest for a Viable Ethos

The disruption of traditional culture and the introduction of Western attitudes and institutions have confronted Middle Eastern societies with the challenge of developing a conceptual-behavioral framework that preserves their own historical legacy and identity while adapting to the universal cosmopolitanism of the modern global system. In Hodgson's view, this situation has created a need for a new moral vision to fill the void left by the disintegration of former allegiances and cultural patterns.[18] This need is made all the more imperative by the prevalence of rigid and simplistic interpretations of Islam and by the breakdown of the secular nationalist order because of ideological deficiencies.

One of the greatest barriers to the construction of a synthesis capable of addressing the demands of modernity is the utopianism apparent in most Middle Eastern political doctrines. Though originally generated by the Islamic concept of the *umma* and its historic mission, which was considerably revised in the medieval period, it was reinforced by nineteenth-century European positivism, which became an important part of nationalist ideologies. The problem inherent in utopianism is that by injecting the idea of perfectability into a political philosophy, it increases the risk of exaggerated interpretations and minimizes flexibility in the theoretical and practical approach to politics. The formulation of finite goals and an acceptance of human imperfection would facilitate the emergence of more realistic and less rigid programs of sociopolitical development. Such an orientation would also stimulate a climate in which the underlying issues can be defined and analyzed.

The most important requirement in constructing a synthesis of Islamic and modern Western culture is a rediscovery of the historical Islam and a redefinition of Islamic values appropriate to the contemporary situation. As Wilfred Cantwell Smith put it, "The fundamental *malaise* of modern Islam is a sense that something has gone wrong with Islamic history. The fundamental problem of modern Muslims is how to rehabilitate that history."[19] It is not a matter of trying to resuscitate the past but of using an accurate reexamination of the Islamic heritage as a principal guideline in the reconstruction of culture and sociopolitical institutions in the present. Hodgson pointed out that

> all cultural action takes place within a setting of tradition, even when in sharpest revolt against particular creative events of the past. As we have seen, tradition is not contrary to progress but a vehicle of it, and one of the problems of Muslims is that on the level of historical action their ties with relevant traditions are so tenuous.[20]

The inability of most contemporary Muslims to correctly interpret the Islamic legacy is a problem of devastating proportions. It is the major obstacle to the evolution of a sound and appropriate cultural composite that could provide the basis of sociopolitical viability in the future. Emmanuel Sivan noted that present-day "Muslims made use of the past—for apologetics, for window dressing—rather than a case in which the past had a creative impact upon the present."[21] Mohammed Arkoun maintained that those representing the secular and Islamic frames of reference in the Middle East are involved in "the manipulation of the symbolic heritage by social performers dominated by a false consciousness of their real historical and cultural situation. . . . Both attitudes reveal the radical inadequacy of the mental equipment applied to analysing Muslim societies and to the definition of a historic action appropriate to their situation."[22]

Arkoun believed that important decisions have to be made about the degree to which Muslims can and should be cut off from their symbolic heritage, on the one hand, and insulated from every foreign influence to the point of enclosing themselves in a single phase of their own history, on the other.[23] He insisted that the secular nationalist and militant neofundamentalist approaches to reform are incapable of dealing with decisions of this kind. What is required is the historian's way of thinking, the methods developed by the school of "applied Islamology," of which Arkoun himself is a leading representative.[24] This approach involves a rediscovery of what the Islamic tradition actually was in history and a reinterpretation of the Quran with specific reference to contemporary issues and challenges.

Marshall Hodgson felt that the general orientation of Islam, contemporary aberrations notwithstanding, is well suited to the related tasks of cultural synthesis and historical reexamination:

> The Islamic heritage was built in a relatively cosmopolitan milieu and its traditionally world-wide outlook should make it possible for Muslims to come to terms with Modern cosmopolitanism. . . .
> . . . [P]erhaps the greatest potential asset of Islam is the frank sense of history that from the beginning has had so large a place in its dialogue. For a willingness to admit seriously that the religious tradition was formed in time and has always had a historical dimension makes it possible to assimilate whatever new insights, into the reality of the heritage and of its creative point of origin, may come through either scholarly research or new spiritual experience.[25]

If the Islamic tradition is based on this kind of cultural and historical vision, as indeed it is, the noticeable lack of such orientation in the present situation is the most tragic reality confronting the Middle East. As Daniel Pipes noted, "By rejecting the medieval synthesis, fundamentalists commit themselves to apply every facet of the Shari'a; they choose to ignore human foibles and a thousand years of experience. . . . If the umma found Islamic precepts unattainable when they were devised a thousand years ago, how could they be applied in the twentieth century?"[26] The neofundamentalists are not alone in the inability to use Islam constructively. The Islamic conservatives and the secularists who are at least nominal Muslims are equally inept. Islamic modernism, which could have provided many helpful guidelines, is a virtually forgotten movement. Though some of its ideas are being revived by such thinkers as Mohammed Arkoun, their impact is very limited and they maintain an extremely low profile because of the sensitive nature of their undertaking.

John Voll distinguished several pairs of contrasting predispositions in Islamic history, opposite sides of which have been emphasized in different contexts.[27] Among these are the tendencies to affirm the diversity of Islamdom and the Islamicate, and the openness of both to acceptance of the achievements of other cultures, as opposed to the conformist and insular position, which seeks to preserve a monolithic and pristine form of Islam. In the contemporary situation, the attitude toward these two alternatives is crucial. The open approach of the Islamic modernists is the only viable option, but the revivalist movement is dominated in the immediate present by the closed and narrow neofundamentalist interpretation. The major challenge of the late twentieth century, therefore, is how to achieve a reorientation of the endeavors to make Islam a vital part of contemporary Muslim life.

As Muslims in the Middle East and elsewhere search for an interpretation of Islam appropriate to contemporary circumstances, they may take increasing interest in the work of the Sudanese Islamic thinker, Mahmoud Mohamed Taha (1909 or 1911–1985).[28] The leader of a group known as the Republicans, Taha elaborated a highly original theology in his book, *The Second Message of Islam.* He distinguished between the concept of Islam developed during the Meccan period of the Prophet's ministry and that formulated after the first *umma* was established in Medina. The original Islam was completely egalitarian and democratic, and it stands as a model of the perfect religious community that will come into being toward the end of time. Medinese Islam, however, was forced by circumstances to abrogate this early manifestation of an ideal to be realized at a much later stage and to institute a sociopolitical system based on *jihad* as the normal approach to the non-Muslim world and a restrictive code of the *sharia* as the only way to preserve the unity and viability of the *umma.* This "first message of Islam," which has determined the institutional basis of Islamdom ever since, represents a postponement rather than a repeal of the Meccan version, which constitutes the "second message of Islam" to be reinstated at a later date.

Taha's notion of a higher humankind of the future, endowed with absolute freedom and a perfected humanity, may appear to some as an example of metaphysical utopianism. Yet its strongly humanistic orientation and open rejection of repressive forms of Islamic practice could, if his theories are accepted as valid, stimulate extensive revision of traditional Islamic jurisprudence and facilitate the cultural synthesis that seems essential for Muslims to accomplish in the modern age.

Both the Islamic and Western traditions contain important elements that can be combined and used in the reconstruction of the cultural, social, and political life of the Middle East. A central theme of this book has been that the highly refined world view that was developed in the early Abbasid period represents a humanistic dimension of Islam that could be instrumental in addressing the current decline of political order in the area. The concept of the unity and harmony of nature and of humankind, developed in Islamic philosophy and portrayed in Islamic art and architecture, can serve as the basis of a fresh approach to the human condition. Recovery of some of the sufi tradition has the potential of stimulating a new sense of spirituality. A reinterpretation of the Friday prayer service and the pilgrimage as the inspirational basis of a doctrine of equality and equity could lead to radical changes in Islamic political thought. The most significant impact of a revived Islamic humanism, however, would be the elimination of a literalistic and largely political understanding of Islam.

The transposition of Western political institutions into the Middle East has permanently changed the area's public orientation. The problem is not that an alien tradition has been introduced but that it has been understood in an imperfect way. Middle Eastern political theorists and practitioners need to reexamine the liberal nationalist idea in its entirety, as it was developed in Europe and the United States. This would help them develop a constitutional framework for their own national movements and minimize the malpractices and instability that have characterized these systems for three generations.

The combination of Islamic and Western traditions in the Middle East has already been undertaken, and this process cannot be reversed. What is subject to change is the way both are interpreted. With proper understanding and implementation of the nobler aspects of each heritage, the cross-fertilization will be relatively free of problems, for these very dimensions are most compatible. What the peoples of the Middle East are groping for is a sociopolitical-intellectual culture of their own, drawn from Islam and parts of other complete traditions and systems but uniquely theirs nevertheless.

The argument that Islam is not Islam unless it conforms to what it was at some particular time and in some particular place should be seriously challenged, since it is demonstrably false. Equally fallacious is the notion that liberal democracy and nationalism can only function in the West. They can operate and have operated elsewhere. They are not the exclusive property of special people. The only requirement is that the necessary institutional structures be in place, and even when they are, they have to be constantly reviewed and reinforced. There is consequently no reason to believe that a satisfactory synthesis cannot be achieved in the Middle East.

Given the now widespread belief in the citizenship principle throughout the area, there will be a growing impatience among the increasingly active and influential populace with misuse of power, whether in the name of nationalism or of Islam. A powerful and ultimately decisive tension has been established in the midst of the body politic. Despite the machinations of political leaders and elites, the demands of the people will eventually prevail. If a ruling class ceases to represent the dominant forces in a society, it will in one way or another be replaced by another elite that is representative in this respect. The same is true for cultural symbols and values.

The Middle East is in transition. Its people have been through painful experiences in the process, and they will encounter more as the quest for a viable ethos moves on to its natural resting place. The end result is difficult to predict, but what does seem reasonably certain is that Islamic humanism and Western liberalism should and will constitute equally important parts of a new tradition that has a distinct Middle Eastern identity. The unidimensional interpretations of Islam and the West produced regimes that frequently violated human rights and dignity to an incredible extent. At some point, the connection between ideology and practice will become clear, and this will be the moment of decision for a troubled area. It is hard to believe that people may make the wrong choices all over again, and it is to be hoped they will not.

Notes

Chapter 1

1. William H. McNeill, *The Rise of the West: A History of the Human Community* (Chicago: University of Chicago Press, 1963), p. 755.

2. Niyazi Berkes, *The Development of Secularism in Turkey* (Montreal: McGill University Press, 1964), pp. 208–218.

3. Albert Hourani, *Arabic Thought in the Liberal Age 1798–1939* (London: Oxford University Press, 1962), pp. 103–160.

4. Arnold Toynbee, *An Historian's Approach to Religion* (New York: Oxford University Press, 1956), pp. 29–39.

Chapter 2

1. Marshall G. S. Hodgson, *The Venture of Islam: Conscience and History in a World Civilization*, 3 vols. (Chicago: University of Chicago Press, 1974), vol. 1, pp. 57–60.

2. See Wael B. Hallaq, "Was the Gate of Ijtihad Closed?" *International Journal of Middle East Studies*, March 1984, pp. 3–41.

3. See Hamilton A. R. Gibb, "An Interpretation of Islamic History," in *Studies on the Civilization of Islam*, ed. Stanford J. Shaw and William R. Polk (Princeton, N.J.: Princeton University Press, 1982), pp. 17–27.

4. Ibid., pp. 13–14.

5. Ira M. Lapidus, "The Separation of State and Religion in the Development of Early Islamic Society," *International Journal of Middle East Studies*, October 1975, p. 364.

6. N. J. Coulson, "The State and the Individual in Islamic Law," in *The Traditional Near East*, ed. J. Stewart-Robinson (Englewood Cliffs, N.J.: Prentice-Hall, 1966), pp. 123–124.

7. Mohammed Arkoun, "Les Droits de l'Homme en Islam," *Recherches et Documents du Centre Thomas More*, December 1984, pp. 15–16.

8. Erwin I. J. Rosenthal, *Political Thought in Medieval Islam: An Introductory Outline* (Cambridge: Cambridge University Press, 1962), pp. 21–51.

9. Ibid., p. 45.

10. See Ira M. Lapidus, *Muslim Cities in the Later Middle Ages* (Cambridge, Mass.: Harvard University Press, 1967), pp. 113–115, 141–142, 183–191.

11. See, for example, Hassan Turabi, "The Islamic State," *Voices of Resurgent Islam,* ed. John L. Esposito (New York: Oxford University Press, 1983), pp. 241–251.

12. Emmanuel Sivan, *Radical Islam: Medieval Theology and Modern Politics* (New Haven, Conn.: Yale University Press, 1985), pp. 94–107.

Chapter 3

1. Niyazi Berkes, ed. and trans., *Turkish Nationalism and Western Civilization: Selected Essays of Ziya Gökalp* (London: Allen and Unwin, 1959), pp. 284–289 and passim; see also Uriel Heyd, *Foundations of Turkish Nationalism: The Life and Teachings of Ziya Gökalp* (London: Luzac and Co. and Harvill Press, 1950), passim.

2. Niyazi Berkes, *The Development of Secularism in Turkey* (Montreal: McGill University Press, 1964), pp. 484–486.

3. Ibid., p. 483.

4. Ibid., p. 341.

5. Ibid., p. 492.

6. Peter Avery, *Modern Iran* (New York: Praeger, 1965), pp. 126–127.

7. Richard W. Cottam, *Nationalism in Iran* (Pittsburgh: University of Pittsburgh Press, 1979), pp. 254–258.

8. See the Paris-based Persian journal, *Sahand.*

9. Albert Hourani, *Arabic Thought in the Liberal Age, 1798–1939* (London: Oxford University Press, 1962), pp. 271–273.

10. Ibid., pp. 298–303.

11. Ibid., p. 162.

12. Nadav Safran, *Egypt in Search of a Political Community: An Analysis of the Intellectual and Political Evolution of Egypt, 1804–1952* (Cambridge, Mass.: Harvard University Press, 1961), pp. 85–90.

13. Ibid., pp. 90–97.

14. Ibid., pp. 144–147.

15. Hourani, op. cit., pp. 361–373.

16. Ibid., p. 285; also see George Antonius, *The Arab Awakening: The Story of the Arab National Movement* (London: Hamish Hamilton, 1938), pp. 108–121; Zeine N. Zeine, *Arab-Turkish Relations and the Emergence of Arab Nationalism* (Beirut: Khayat's, 1958), pp. 73–116.

17. Antonius, op. cit., p. 153.

18. William L. Cleveland, *The Making of an Arab Nationalist: Ottomanism and Arabism in the Thought of Sati' al-Husri* (Princeton, N.J.: Princeton University Press, 1971), p. 70.

19. Ibid., pp. 96–97.

20. Ibid., p. 89.

21. Ibid., pp. 170–171.

22. Ibid., p. 90.

23. Sylvia Haim, ed., *Arab Nationalism: An Anthology* (Berkeley and Los Angeles, Calif.: University of California Press, 1962), pp. 55–57.

24. Ibid., p. 63.

25. Malcolm Kerr, "The Political Outlook in the Local Arena," in Abraham S. Becker, Bert Hansen, and Malcolm H. Kerr, *The Economics and Politics of the Middle East* (New York: American Elsevier, 1975), pp. 41–54.

26. Fouad Ajami, "The End of Pan-Arabism," *Foreign Affairs*, winter 1978–1979.

Chapter 4

1. Albert Hourani, *Arabic Thought in the Liberal Age, 1798–1939* (London: Oxford University Press, 1962), pp. 114–117.

2. Ibid., p. 138.

3. Charles C. Adams, *Islam and Modernism in Egypt: A Study of the Modern Reform Movement Inaugurated by Muhammad 'Abduh* (New York: Russell and Russell, 1968), p. 174.

4. Hourani, op. cit., p. 143.

5. Marshall G. S. Hodgson, *The Venture of Islam: Conscience and History in a World Civilization*, 3 vols. (Chicago: University of Chicago Press, 1974), vol. 1, p. 97.

6. Hourani, op. cit., p. 136.

7. See Niyazi Berkes, *The Development of Secularism in Turkey* (Montreal: McGill University Press, 1964), pp. 209–218; Şerif Mardin, *The Genesis of Young Ottoman Thought: A Study in the Modernization of Turkish Political Ideas* (Princeton, N.J.: Princeton University Press, 1962), pp. 283–336.

8. Hourani, op. cit., pp. 183–189.

9. G. H. Jansen, *Militant Islam* (New York: Harper and Row, 1979), p. 124.

10. Ibid., p. 127.

11. See Fouad Ajami, *The Arab Predicament: Arab Political Thought and Practice Since 1967* (New York: Cambridge University Press, 1981), pp. 170–171; Nikki R. Keddie, *Roots of Revolution: An Interpretive History of Modern Iran* (New Haven, Conn.: Yale University Press, 1981), p. 183.

12. See Ajami, op. cit., p. 176; John O. Voll, "The Sudanese Mahdi: Frontier Fundamentalist," *International Journal of Middle East Studies*, May 1979, pp. 145–166; John O. Voll, "Wahhabism and Mahdism: Alternative Styles of Islamic Renewals," *Arab Studies Quarterly*, spring 1982, pp. 110–126.

13. Voll, "Wahhabism and Mahdism," op. cit., p. 125.

14. Richard D. Mitchell, *The Society of Muslim Brothers* (London: Oxford University Press, 1969), p. 7.

15. Ibid., pp. 209–211.

16. Ibid., pp. 224–226.

17. Ibid., p. 234.

18. Ibid., p. 238.

19. Kemal Karpat, ed., *Political and Social Thought in the Contemporary Middle East* (New York: Praeger, 1982), p. 100.

20. Mitchell, op. cit., p. 264.

21. Ibid., pp. 265–266.

22. Ibid., p. 270.

23. Yvonne Y. Haddad, "Sayyid Qutb: Ideologue of the Islamic Revival," in *Voices of Resurgent Islam*, ed. John L. Esposito (New York: Oxford University Press, 1983), pp. 93–94.

24. Ibid., pp. 67–68.

25. Ibid., pp. 83–87.

26. See Sayyid Abul A'la Maududi, *A Short History of the Revivalist Movement in Islam*, trans. Al-Ashari, 6th ed. (Lahore: Islamic Publications Limited, 1986), pp. 5–34.

27. Sayyid Qutb, *Milestones* (Cedar Rapids, Iowa: Unity Publishing Co., 1981), p. 20.

28. Ibid., p. 21.

29. Ibid., p. 46.

30. Ibid., pp. 62, 70.

31. Ibid., p. 82.

32. Ibid., pp. 115–116.

33. Ibid., p. 124.

34. Ibid., p. 131.

35. Ibid., p. 111.

36. Ajami, op. cit., pp. 52–62.

37. Gilles Kepel, *The Prophet and Pharaoh: Muslim Extremism in Egypt*, trans. Jon Rothschild (London: Al Saqi Books, 1985), pp. 172–190.

38. Mitchell, op. cit., pp. 36–37.

39. Ibid., p. 331.

40. Hamid Enayat, *Modern Islamic Political Thought* (Austin: University of Texas Press, 1982), pp. 93–99.

41. Edward Mortimer, *Faith and Power: The Politics of Islam* (New York: Random House, 1982), p. 349.

42. Keddie, op. cit., p. 154.

43. Ibid., p. 158; Mortimer, op. cit., p. 318; Michael Fischer, *Iran: From Religious Dispute to Revolution* (Cambridge, Mass.: Harvard University Press, 1980), pp. 123–124.

44. See Kambiz Afrachteh, "Iran," in *The Politics of Islamic Reassertion*, ed. Mohammed Ayoob (London: Croom Helm, 1981), pp. 106–109; Yann Richard, "Contemporary Shii Thought," in Keddie, op. cit., pp. 205–214; Mortimer, op. cit., pp. 326–334; Michael Fischer, "Imam Khomeini: Four Levels of Understanding," in Esposito, op. cit., pp. 150–174.

45. Fischer, "Imam Khomeini," in Esposito, op. cit., p. 164.

46. See Hamid Algar, ed. and trans., *Islam and Revolution: Writings and Declarations of Imam Khomeini* (Berkeley, Calif.: Mizan Press, 1981), pp. 25–166.

47. Fischer, "Imam Khomeini," in Esposito, op. cit., p. 160.

48. Richard, "Contemporary Shii Thought," in Keddie, op. cit., pp. 203–205.

49. See ibid., pp. 215–225; Enayat, op. cit., pp. 155–158; Abdulaziz Sachedina, "Ali Shariati: Ideologue of the Iranian Revolution," in Esposito, op. cit., pp. 191–214.

50. See Richard, "Contemporary Shii Thought," in Keddie, op. cit., pp. 225–228; Mortimer, op. cit., pp. 346–348.

51. Keddie, op. cit., pp. 183–185.

Chapter 5

1. Malcolm Kerr, "The Political Outlook in the Local Arena," in Abraham Becker, Bert Hansen, and Malcolm Kerr, *The Economics and Politics of the Middle East* (New York: American Elsevier, 1975), p. 42.

2. Ibid., pp. 43–45.

3. Robert Springborg, "Egypt, Syria and Iraq," in *The Politics of Islamic Reassertion*, ed. Mohammed Ayoob (London: Croom Helm, 1981), pp. 35–38.

4. Saad Eddin Ibrahim, "Anatomy of Egypt's Militant Islamic Groups: Methodological Note and Preliminary Findings," *International Journal of Middle East Studies*, December 1980, pp. 423–453.

5. See comments on this translation in *Middle East Journal*, winter 1983, p. 27; autumn 1983, p. 754; spring 1984, p. 386.

6. Edward Mortimer, *Faith and Power: The Politics of Islam* (New York: Random House, 1982), pp. 290–292.

7. R. Hrair Dekmejian, *Islam in Revolution: Fundamentalism in the Arab World* (Syracuse, N.Y.: Syracuse University Press, 1985), p. 102.

8. Saad Eddin Ibrahim, "Militant Islam Joins the Mainstream," *Arabia*, April 1984, p. 69.

9. Ibid., p. 68; Dekmejian, op. cit., p. 61; Nazih Ayubi, "The Political Revival of Islam: The Case of Egypt," *International Journal of Middle East Studies*, December 1980, p. 494.

10. Ibrahim, op. cit., p. 69.

11. Dekmejian, op. cit., p. 112.

12. Mortimer, op. cit., p. 264.

13. See Raymond Hinnebusch, "The Islamic Movement in Syria: Sectarian Conflict and Urban Rebellion in an Authoritarian-Populist Regime," in *Islamic Resurgence in the Arab World*, ed. Ali Dessouki (New York: Praeger, 1982), pp. 138–141.

14. Springborg, op. cit., p. 41.

15. See Hinnebusch, op. cit., pp. 150–152.

16. Mortimer, op. cit., p. 269; Dekmejian, op. cit., pp. 116–118.

17. Dekmejian, op. cit., p. 130.

18. Hanna Batatu, "Iraq's Underground Shi'a Movements: Characteristics, Causes and Prospects," *Middle East Journal*, autumn 1981, pp. 588–589.

19. Dekmejian, op. cit., pp. 131–133.

20. Batatu, op. cit., pp. 591–592.

21. Wilhelm Dietl, *Holy War*, trans. Martha Humphreys (New York: Macmillan, 1984), pp. 155–158.

22. Marius K. Deeb, *Militant Islamic Movements in Lebanon: Origins, Social Basis, and Ideology* (Washington, D.C.: Center for Contemporary Arab Studies, 1986), pp. 12–17.

23. James A. Bill, "Resurgent Islam in the Persian Gulf," *Foreign Affairs*, fall 1984, pp. 108–109.

24. Dekmejian, op. cit., p. 140 (based on a reference to William Ochsenwald, "Saudi Arabia and the Islamic Revival," *International Journal of Middle East Studies*, August 1981, p. 274).

25. Ibid., pp. 141–144; Frank Sankari, "Islam and Politics in Saudi Arabia," in Dessouki, op. cit., pp. 190–191.

26. Dekmejian, op. cit., pp. 149–157.

27. Jean-Claude Vatin, "Revival in the Maghreb: Islam as an Alternate Political Language," in Dessouki, op. cit., p. 221.

28. Mohammed Arkoun, "Positivism and Tradition in an Islamic Perspective: Kemalism," trans. R. Scott Walker, *Diogenes*, fall 1984, p. 95.

29. Mortimer, op. cit., pp. 277–283.

30. Ibid., p. 183.

31. James A. Bill, "Power and Religion in Revolutionary Iran," *Middle East Journal*, winter 1982, p. 27.

32. Ibid., p. 25.

33. Michael Fischer, *Iran: From Religious Dispute to Revolution* (Cambridge, Mass.: Harvard University Press, 1980), pp. 124–127.

34. Shaul Bakhash, *The Reign of the Ayatollahs: Iran and the Islamic Revolution* (New York: Basic Books, 1984), pp. 45–48.

35. Bill, "Power and Religion in Revolutionary Iran," op. cit., pp. 24–25.

36. Mortimer, op. cit., pp. 148–149.

37. Ibid., p. 151.

38. Turker Alkan, "The National Salvation Party in Turkey," in *Islam and Politics in the Modern Middle East*, ed. Metin Heper and Raphael Israeli (New York: St. Martin's Press, 1984), pp. 82–83.

39. Ibid., pp. 85–86.

40. Ibid., pp. 87–88.

41. Mortimer, op. cit., p. 156.

42. Nicholas S. Ludington, "Turkish Islam and the Secular State," *The Muslim World Today*, Occasional Paper no. 1 (Washington, D.C.: American Institute for Islamic Affairs, 1984), p. 2.

43. Ibid., pp. 9–11.

Chapter 6

1. Based on an interview with the editorial staff of the nationalist publication, *Sahand*, Paris, September 26, 1985.

2. Amir Taheri, *The Spirit of Allah: Khomeini and the Islamic Revolution* (Bethesda, Md.: Adler and Adler, 1986), pp. 97–98.

3. Ibid., pp. 101–102, 107.

4. Ibid., pp. 103–118.

5. Ibid., pp. 229–231.

6. Shaul Bakhash, *The Reign of the Ayatollahs: Iran and the Islamic Revolution* (New York: Basic Books, 1984), p. 19.

7. See Hamid Algar, ed. and trans., *Islam and Revolution: Writings and Declarations of Imam Khomeini* (Berkeley, Calif.: Mizan Press, 1981).

8. Ibid., pp. 204–207.

9. Nikki R. Keddie, *Roots of Revolution: An Interpretive History of Modern Iran* (New Haven, Conn.: Yale University Press, 1981), pp. 242–243.

10. Bakhash, op. cit., p. 45.

11. Ibid., pp. 49–51.

12. Based on an interview with Shahpur Baktiar, Paris, September 27, 1985.

13. Michael Fischer, *Iran: From Religious Dispute to Revolution* (Cambridge, Mass.: Harvard University Press, 1980), p. 212.

14. Bakhash, op. cit., pp. 64–66.

15. Ibid., p. 63.

16. Fischer, op. cit., p. 220. Interview with Abul Hasan Bani-Sadr, Paris, September 25, 1985.

17. Bakhash, op. cit., pp. 71–91.

18. Ibid., p. 99.

19. Ibid., p. 104.

20. Sepehr Zabih, *Iran Since the Revolution* (Baltimore, Md.: Johns Hopkins University Press, 1982), pp. 65–68.

21. Bakhash, op. cit., pp. 146–147, 153–159, 163–164.

22. Zabih, op. cit., pp. 138–158.

23. *Amnesty International Report 1982*, p. 323.

24. Taheri, op. cit., p. 278.

25. *Amnesty International Reports 1980–1986*.

26. Taheri, op. cit., p. 278; *Amnesty International Report 1982*, p. 324.

27. Taheri, op. cit., p. 278. References cited are *Sobh Azadegan*, June 20, 1981, and *The Guardian*, June 24, 1981.

28. *Amnesty International Report 1982*, p. 324. Reference cited is *The Times*, London, September 21, 1981.

29. See *Amnesty International's Written Statement on Human Rights in Iran to the Political Affairs Committee of the European Parliament (November 28, 1985)*; and *Amnesty International Reports 1982–1985*.

30. Taheri, op. cit., p. 278.

31. Based on figures of Amnesty International.

32. Taheri, op. cit., p. 117. Quoted by Sheikh Ali Tehrani in *Erchad*, Paris, January 1985.

33. Rouhollah K. Ramazani, *Revolutionary Iran: Challenge and Response in the Middle East* (Baltimore, Md.: Johns Hopkins University Press, 1986), p. 24.

34. Taheri, op. cit., pp. 273–274.

35. Associated Press, "Khomeini Calls War Crusade," *Washington Post*, February 11, 1987.

36. Ramazani, op. cit., pp. 3–19.

37. Adeed Dawisha, "Iraq: The West's Opportunity," *Foreign Policy*, winter 1980–1981, pp. 145–146.

38. *War in the Gulf: A Staff Report Prepared for the Committee on Foreign Relations, U.S. Senate* (Washington, D.C.: Government Printing Office, August

1984); Adeed Dawisha, "The Iranian Revolution: The Thrill Is Gone," Outlook Section, *Washington Post*, November 23, 1986, p. 2.

39. Ramazani, op. cit., p. 19.

40. Dawisha, "The Iranian Revolution: The Thrill Is Gone," op. cit., p. 2.

41. Taheri, op. cit., p. 286.

42. Ibid.

43. Ibid.

44. Loren Jenkins, "Iranian Power Struggle Said to Be Escalating," *Washington Post*, February 4, 1987.

Chapter 7

1. John G. A. Pocock, *The Machiavellian Moment: Florentine Political Thought and the Atlantic Republican Tradition* (Princeton, N.J.: Princeton University Press, 1975), pp. 506–552.

2. Mohammed Arkoun, "Positivism and Tradition in an Islamic Perspective: Kemalism," trans. R. Scott Walker, *Diogenes*, fall 1984, p. 89.

3. Daniel Pipes, *In the Path of God: Islam and Political Power* (New York: Basic Books, 1983), p. 115.

4. Ibid., pp. 116–119.

5. Ibid., p. 199.

6. Marshall G. S. Hodgson, *The Venture of Islam: Conscience and History in a World Civilization*, 3 vols. (Chicago: University of Chicago Press, 1974), vol. 3, p. 167.

7. Ibid., vol. 3, pp. 200–201.

8. Ibid., vol. 3, pp. 274–275.

9. Ibid., vol. 3, p. 275.

10. Gilles Kepel, *The Prophet and Pharaoh: Muslim Extremism in Egypt*, trans. Jon Rothschild (London: Al Saqi Books, 1985), p. 228.

11. Pipes, op. cit., pp. 128–130.

12. Emmanuel Sivan, *Radical Islam: Medieval Theology and Modern Politics* (New Haven, Conn.: Yale University Press, 1985), p. 102.

13. Ibid., pp. 95–96.

14. Ibid., pp. 124–125.

15. Ibid., p. 186.

16. Pipes, op. cit., p. 130.

17. Ibid., p. 141.

18. Hodgson, op. cit., vol. 3, p. 436.

19. Wilfred Cantwell Smith, *Islam in Modern History* (Princeton, N.J.: Princeton University Press, 1957), p. 41.

20. Hodgson, op. cit., vol. 3, p. 431.

21. Sivan, op. cit., p. ix.

22. Arkoun, op. cit., p. 93.

23. Ibid., p. 95.

24. Mohammed Arkoun, *Pour une critique de la raison islamique* (Paris: Maisonneuve and Larose, 1984), pp. 43–63. Also based on an interview with Mohammed Arkoun, Paris, July 7, 1986.

25. Hodgson, op. cit., vol. 3, pp. 436–437.

26. Pipes, op. cit., p. 135.

27. John O. Voll, "The Sudanese Mahdi: Frontier Fundamentalist," *International Journal of Middle East Studies*, May 1979, pp. 147–152.

28. See Mahmoud Mohamed Taha, *The Second Message of Islam*, trans. Abdullahi Ahmed An-Na'im (Syracuse, N.Y.: Syracuse University Press, 1987).

Bibliography

Books

Adams, Charles C. *Islam and Modernism in Egypt: A Study of the Modern Reform Movement Inaugurated by Muhammad 'Abduh.* New York: Russell and Russell, 1968.

Ajami, Fouad. *The Arab Predicament: Arab Political Thought and Practice Since 1967.* New York: Cambridge University Press, 1981.

Algar, Hamid, ed. and trans. *Islam and Revolution: Writings and Declarations of Imam Khomeini.* Berkeley, Calif.: Mizan Press, 1981.

Amnesty International. *Amnesty International Reports 1980–1986.*

————. *Amnesty International's Written Statement on Human Rights in Iran to the Political Affairs Committee of the European Parliament.* November 28, 1985.

Antonius, George. *The Arab Awakening: The Story of the Arab National Movement.* London: Hamish Hamilton, 1938.

Arkoun, Mohammed. *Pour une critique de la raison islamique.* Paris: Maisonneuve and Larose, 1984.

Avery, Peter. *Modern Iran.* New York: Praeger, 1965.

Ayoob, Mohammed, ed. *The Politics of Islamic Reassertion.* London: Croom Helm, 1981.

Bakhash, Shaul. *The Reign of the Ayatollahs: Iran and the Islamic Revolution.* New York: Basic Books, 1984.

Berkes, Niyazi. *The Development of Secularism in Turkey.* Montreal: McGill University Press, 1964.

Berkes, Niyazi, ed. and trans. *Turkish Nationalism and Western Civilization: Selected Essays of Ziya Gökalp.* London: Allen and Unwin, 1959.

Cleveland, William L. *The Making of an Arab Nationalist: Ottomanism and Arabism in the Thought of Sati' al-Husri.* Princeton, N.J.: Princeton University Press, 1971.

Cottam, Richard W. *Nationalism in Iran.* Pittsburgh: University of Pittsburgh Press, 1979.

Deeb, Marius K. *Militant Islamic Movements in Lebanon: Origins, Social Basis, and Ideology.* Washington, D.C.: Center for Contemporary Arab Studies, 1986.

Dekmejian, R. Hrair. *Islam in Revolution: Fundamentalism in the Arab World.* Syracuse, N.Y.: Syracuse University Press, 1985.

Dessouki, Ali, ed. *Islamic Resurgence in the Arab World.* New York: Praeger, 1982.

Dietl, Wilhelm. *Holy War,* trans. Martha Humphreys. New York: Macmillan, 1984.

Enayat, Hamid. *Modern Islamic Political Thought.* Austin: University of Texas Press, 1982.

Esposito, John L., ed. *Voices of Resurgent Islam.* New York: Oxford University Press, 1983.

Fischer, Michael. *Iran: From Religious Dispute to Revolution.* Cambridge, Mass.: Harvard University Press, 1980.

Gibb, Hamiltin A. R. *Studies on the Civilization of Islam,* ed. Stanford J. Shaw and William R. Polk. Princeton, N.J.: Princeton University Press, 1982.

Haim, Sylvia, ed. *Arab Nationalism: An Anthology.* Berkeley and Los Angeles: University of California Press, 1962.

Heper, Metin, and Raphael Israeli, eds. *Islam and Politics in the Modern Middle East.* New York: St. Martin's Press, 1984.

Heyd, Uriel. *Foundations of Turkish Nationalism: The Life and Teachings of Ziya Gökalp.* London: Luzac and Co. and Harvill Press, 1950.

Hodgson, Marshall G. S. *The Venture of Islam: Conscience and History in a World Civilization,* 3 vols. Chicago: University of Chicago Press, 1974.

Hourani, Albert. *Arabic Thought in the Liberal Age, 1798–1939.* London: Oxford University Press, 1962.

Jansen, G. H. *Militant Islam.* New York: Harper and Row, 1979.

Karpat, Kemal, ed. *Political and Social Thought in the Contemporary Middle East.* New York: Praeger, 1982.

Keddie, Nikki R. *Roots of Revolution: An Interpretive History of Modern Iran.* New Haven, Conn.: Yale University Press, 1981.

Kepel, Gilles. *The Prophet and Pharaoh: Muslim Extremism in Egypt,* trans. Jon Rothschild. London: Al Saqi Books, 1985.

Lapidus, Ira M. *Muslim Cities in the Later Middle Ages.* Cambridge, Mass.: Harvard Univeristy Press, 1967.

Mardin, Şerif. *The Genesis of Young Ottoman Thought: A Study in the Modernization of Turkish Political Ideas.* Princeton, N.J.: Princeton University Press, 1962.

Maududi, Sayyid Abul A'la. *A Short History of the Revivalist Movement in Islam,* trans. Al-Ashari, 6th ed. Lahore: Islamic Publications Limited, 1986.

McNeill, William H. *The Rise of the West: A History of the Human Community.* Chicago: University of Chicago Press, 1963.

Mitchell, Richard D. *The Society of Muslim Brothers.* London: Oxford University Press, 1969.

Mortimer, Edward. *Faith and Power: The Politics of Islam.* New York: Random House, 1982.

Pipes, Daniel. *In the Path of God: Islam and Political Power.* New York: Basic Books, 1983.

Pocock, John G. A. *The Machiavellian Moment: Florentine Political Thought and the Atlantic Republican Tradition.* Princeton, N.J.: Princeton University Press, 1975.

Qutb, Sayyid. *Milestones.* Cedar Rapids, Iowa: Unity Publishing, 1981.

Ramazani, Rouhollah K. *Revolutionary Iran: Challenge and Response in the Middle East.* Baltimore, Md.: Johns Hopkins University Press, 1986.

Rosenthal, Erwin, I. J. *Political Thought in Medieval Islam: An Introductory Outline.* Cambridge: Cambridge University Press, 1962.

Safran, Nadav. *Egypt in Search of a Political Community: An Analysis of the Intellectual and Political Evolution of Egypt, 1804–1952*. Cambridge, Mass.: Harvard University Press, 1961.

Sivan, Emmanuel. *Radical Islam: Medieval Theology and Modern Politics*. New Haven, Conn.: Yale University Press, 1985.

Smith, Wilfred Cantwell. *Islam in Modern History*. Princeton, N.J.: Princeton University Press, 1957.

Steward-Robinson, J. *The Traditional Near East*. Englewood Cliffs, N.J.: Prentice-Hall, 1966.

Taha, Mahmoud Mohamed. *The Second Message of Islam*, trans. Abdullahi Ahmed An-Na'im. Syracuse, N.Y.: Syracuse University Press, 1987.

Taheri, Amir. *The Spirit of Allah: Khomeini and the Islamic Revolution*. Bethesda, Md.: Adler and Adler, 1986.

Toynbee, Arnold. *An Historian's Approach to Religion*. New York: Oxford University Press, 1956.

War in the Gulf: A Staff Report Prepared for the Committee on Foreign Relations, U.S. Senate. Washington, D.C.: Government Printing Office, 1984.

Zabih, Sepehr. *Iran Since the Revolution*. Baltimore, Md.: Johns Hopkins University Press, 1982.

Zeine, Zeine N. *Arab-Turkish Relations and the Emergence of Arab Nationalism*. Beirut: Khayat's, 1958.

Articles and Chapters

Afrachteh, Kambiz. "Iran," in *The Politics of Islamic Reassertion*, ed. Mohammed Ayoob. London: Croom Helm, 1981.

Ajami, Fouad. "The End of Pan-Arabism," *Foreign Affairs*, winter, 1978–1979.

Alkan, Turker. "The National Salvation Party in Turkey," in *Islam and Politics in the Modern Middle East*, ed. Metin Heper and Raphael Israeli. New York: St. Martin's Press, 1984.

Arkoun, Mohammed. "Les Droits de l'Homme en Islam," *Recherches et Documents du Centre Thomas More*, December 1984.

Arkoun, Mohammed. "Positivism and Tradition in an Islamic Perspective; Kemalism," trans. R. Scott Walker, *Diogenes*, fall 1984.

Associated Press. "Khomeini Calls War Crusade," *Washington Post*, February 11, 1987.

Ayubi, Nazih. "The Political Revival of Islam: The Case of Egypt," *International Journal of Middle East Studies*, December 1980.

Batatu, Hanna. "Iraq's Underground Shi'a Movements: Characteristics, Causes and Prospects," *Middle East Journal*, autumn 1981.

Bill, James A. "Power and Religion in Revolutionary Iran," *Middle East Journal*, winter 1982.

———. "Resurgent Islam in the Persian Gulf," *Foreign Affairs*, fall 1984.

Coulson, N. J. "The State and the Individual in Islamic Law," in *The Traditional Near East*, ed. J. Stewart-Robinson. Englewood Cliffs, N.J.: Prentice-Hall, 1966.

Dawisha, Adeed. "The Iranian Revolution: The Thrill Is Gone," Outlook Section, *Washington Post*, November 23, 1986.

_____ . "Iraq: The West's Opportunity," *Foreign Policy*, winter 1980–1981.

Fischer, Michael. "Imam Khomeini: Four Levels of Understanding," in *Voices of Resurgent Islam*, ed. John L. Esposito. New York: Oxford University Press, 1983.

Gibb, Hamiltin A. R. "An Interpretation of Islamic History," in *Studies on the Civilization of Islam*, ed. Stanford J. Shaw and William R. Polk. Princeton, N.J.: Princeton University Press, 1982.

Haddad, Yvonne Y. "Sayyid Qutb: Ideologue of the Islamic Revival," in *Voices of Resurgent Islam*, ed. John L. Esposito. New York: Oxford University Press, 1983.

Hallaq, Wael B. "Was the Gate of Ijtihad Closed?" *International Journal of Middle East Studies*, March 1984.

Hinnebusch, Raymond. "The Islamic Movement in Syria: Sectarian Conflict and Urban Rebellion in an Authoritarian-Populist Regime," in *Islamic Resurgence in the Arab World*, ed. Ali Dessouki. New York: Praeger, 1982.

Ibrahim, Saad Eddin. "Anatomy of Egypt's Militant Islamic Groups: Methodological Note and Preliminary Findings," *International Journal of Middle East Studies*, December 1980.

_____ . "Militant Islam Joins the Mainstream," *Arabia*, April 1984.

Jenkins, Loren. "Iranian Power Struggle Said to Be Escalating," *Washington Post*, February 4, 1987.

Kerr, Malcolm. "The Political Outlook in the Local Arena," in *The Economics and Politics of the Middle East* by Abraham S. Becker, Bert Hansen, and Malcolm H. Kerr. New York: American Elsevier, 1975.

Lapidus, Ira M. "The Separation of State and Religion in the Development of Early Islamic Society," *International Journal of Middle East Studies*, October 1975.

Ludington, Nicholas S. "Turkish Islam and the Secular State," in *The Muslim World Today*, Occasional Paper no. 1. Washington, D.C.: American Institute for Islamic Affairs, 1984.

Ochsenwald, William. "Saudi Arabia and the Islamic Revival," *International Journal of Middle East Studies*, August 1981.

Richard, Yann. "Contemporary Shii Thought," in *Roots of Revolution: An Interpretive History of Modern Iran*, by Nikki R. Keddie. New Haven, Conn.: Yale University Press, 1981.

Sachedina, Abdulaziz. "Ali Shariati: Ideologue of the Iranian Revolution," in *Voices of Resurgent Islam*, ed. John L. Esposito. New York: Oxford University Press, 1983.

Sankari, Frank. "Islam and Politics in Saudi Arabia," in *Islamic Resurgence in the Arab World*, ed. Ali Dessouki. New York: Praeger, 1982.

Springborg, Robert. "Egypt, Syria and Iraq," in *The Politics of Islamic Reassertion*, ed. Mohammed Ayoob. London: Croom Helm, 1981.

Turabi, Hassan. "The Islamic State," in *Voices of Resurgent Islam*, ed. John L. Esposito. New York: Oxford University Press, 1983.

Vatin, Jean-Claude. "Revival in the Maghreb: Islam as an Alternative Political Language," in *Islamic Resurgence in the Arab World*, ed. Ali Dessouki. New York: Praeger, 1982.

Voll, John O. "The Sudanese Mahdi: Frontier Fundamentalist," *International Journal of Middle East Studies*, May 1979.

―――― . "Wahhabism and Mahdism: Alternative Styles of Islamic Renewals," *Arab Studies Quarterly*, spring 1982.

Index